OCEAN CITY

MICHAEL MORGAN

OCEAN CITY

GOING DOWN THE OCEAN

Charleston · London

THE
History
PRESS

Published by The History Press
Charleston, SC 29403
www.historypress.net

Copyright © 2011 by Michael Morgan
All rights reserved

First published 2011

Manufactured in the United States

ISBN 978.1.60949.162.8

Library of Congress Cataloging-in-Publication Data

Morgan, Michael, 1943-
Ocean City : going down the ocean / Michael Morgan.
p. cm.
Includes bibliographical references.
ISBN 978-1-60949-162-8
1. Ocean City (Md.)--History--Anecdotes. I. Title.
F189.O2M67 2011
975.2'21--dc22
2011003222

CONTENTS

PREFACE

More than half a century ago, I was a youngster living in Baltimore when I first heard the exchange, "What are you doing this summer hon?…I am going down the ocean." Since that time, I have gone down the ocean many times, bought my first condominium and finally made my home in Ocean City. Living amid the resort's rich history, it has been easy to appreciate why Ocean City's sun, surf and sand have had such an enduring appeal.

This book would not have been possible without the assistance of the kind folks who toil in the libraries, archives and museums of the coastal region. I would like to thank the staff of the Snow Hill Public Library, Teresa Travatello of the Ocean Pines Association and Randy L. Goss at the Delaware Public Archives for their help in securing images for this book. I would also like to thank Linda Mitchell and Carol Rechner for allowing me to use images from their family collections. In particular, thanks go to Claire Otterbein and the staff of the Julia A. Purnell Museum for their help in producing this book. The museum is home to more than ten thousand artifacts and photographs that highlight local history, including artwork from the museum's namesake.

Thanks also to Hannah Cassilly at The History Press for her support and encouragement for this project. I would also like to thank my son, Tom, a former member of the Ocean City Beach Patrol, and his wife, Karla, a native of the coastal region and an expert on Ocean City real estate, for their advice and support.

The Ocean City boardwalk. *Photo by Michael Morgan.*

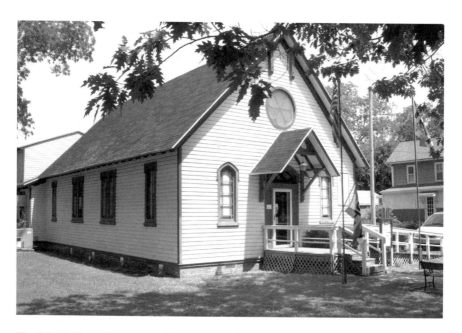

The Julia A. Purnell Museum in Snow Hill. *Photo by Michael Morgan.*

Finally, I would like to thank my patient wife, Madelyn, who encouraged me to write this book knowing that she would spend countless hours correcting my spelling, punctuation and grammar. She read every word numerous times; without her help, this book would not have been possible. Whatever errors remain are mine.

CHAPTER 1

ROSES, VIOLETS AND LILIES

VERRAZANO SMELLS THE ROSES

Ocean City, Maryland, sits on a broad ribbon of sand that begins with the inlet and stretches northward to Delaware and beyond; it was not always so. The sands of the Maryland coast are constantly in motion as they are buffeted about by the winds and waves. Inlets appear and disappear, and chunks of the beach become islands, only to be reattached to the mainland decades later. Five centuries ago, several inlets led from the Atlantic Ocean to the coastal bays; one of the most important of these waterways was Sinepuxent Inlet. For many years, this inlet cut across the barrier island south of Ocean City, and in 1524, the first European ship, captained by Giovanni da Verrazano, cautiously made its way through the narrow waterway.

Born in Florence, Italy, in the late fifteenth century, Verrazano was only twelve years old when Christopher Columbus made his historic voyage across the Atlantic Ocean. Verrazano's parents were associated with the silk merchants of southern France, and he was sent to France for his education. Buoyed by his family's fortune, Verrazano became a gentleman of some standing in France. After several sea voyages, he had become a competent navigator.

In the early sixteenth century, the overland trade route between Europe and China was threatened by unrest in the area that is now the Middle East. European captains who had honed their navigational skills in the Mediterranean Sea turned to the Atlantic in search of an all-water route to the Orient. In 1524, the king of France commissioned Verrazano to cross the Atlantic in an effort to find a navigable route to China.

The voyages of Columbus had unleashed a flood of expeditions to Central and South America, but only a few probing voyages had been made to the north. Except for the explorations by Ponce de León in Florida and John Cabot in Newfoundland, North America had been largely ignored. When Verrazano set sail from France in a small sailing ship named *La Dauphine*, he planned to explore the unknown waters that had been snubbed by less intrepid mariners.

Setting out in the spring of 1524, Verrazano caught the prevailing easterly winds that drove *La Dauphine* across the Atlantic. After making landfall along the Carolina coast, Verrazano headed north. Given his chance to discover new lands, the eager explorer turned cautious. As an experienced mariner, he feared sailing in waters where the shoals and shallows had not been charted. The great "Admiral of the Ocean Sea," Christopher Columbus, had lost the *Santa Maria* to such shoals near Haiti in 1492. To avoid these hazards, Verrazano followed the practice of a careful captain and kept *La Dauphine* well away from the beach to ensure that his ship would be in deep water. When he reached the Outer Banks of North Carolina, the explorer remained so far from the coast that he mistook the broad expanse of the Pamlico Sound for the Pacific Ocean.

After he reached the coast of the Delmarva Peninsula, Verrazano may have regained some of the courage that had driven him to become an explorer. Historians debate the exact locations that Verrazano visited on this voyage, but it appears that he entered Chincoteague Bay from the south and sailed northward until he anchored in the vicinity of Sinepuxent Inlet. Assured that the inlet would provide him with a safe route back to the Atlantic Ocean, the explorer anchored *La Dauphine* a safe distance from shore.

Verrazano and several crewmen boarded a small boat and rowed to the mainland. Like many tourists, the first European to visit the Ocean City area penned a description of his trip to folks back home, which in this case included the king of France: "We came…to another land, which appeared very beautiful and full of the largest forests. We approached it, and going ashore with twenty men, we went back from the coast about two leagues, and found that the people had fled and hid themselves in the woods for fear."

The Native Americans whom the Italian explorer encountered were members of one of the Algonquin tribes that lived on the mainland west of the coastal bays. These tribes bore names such as Pocomoke, Chincoteague and Assateague, which have become attached to geographic features of the coastal region. Etymologists have struggled to determine the meanings of these names. Most etymologists believe that Assateague means "the place

Giovanni da Verrazano arrived off the Worcester County coast in the sixteenth century, three centuries before Ocean City was established. *Courtesy of the Julia A. Purnell Museum.*

across," but other word specialists render the meaning as "the river across"; a third school interprets Assateague to mean "brown or yellow river."

Assawoman is another Native American place name that has bedeviled etymologists, and there is little consensus on its meaning. Some have suggested that Assawoman means "fishing place," but others maintain that the evidence is too flimsy to make that assumption. Etymologists have also wrestled with Chincoteague, and again, they are far from unanimous. Some word experts have suggested that it means "a place where fish and oysters are caught," but the more accepted translation is "a large stream." This indicates that Chincoteague Bay may have received this Native American name first, and then the name was applied to Chincoteague Island.

The same confusion of land and water applies to Sinepuxent. The northern extension of Chincoteague Bay is known as Sinepuxent Bay. In addition, the neck of land that juts into northern Chincoteague Bay is also known as Sinepuxent Neck. This stony neck of land may have been the source for the Sinepuxent (believed to mean "stony swamp") place name. Just as etymologists have varying explanations for the meanings of some of the Native American words, the spelling of these terms has varied over the years. For example, "Sinepuxent" sometimes appears as "Synapuxant" or "Synepuxent."

For most of the year, the Native Americans encountered by Verrazano lived in homes constructed of wood and bark; during the summer months,

Coastal Native Americans lived in permanent houses made of wood and bark. *Courtesy of the Julia A. Purnell Museum.*

they sometimes moved to the beach. Although Europeans had been exploring American waters for three decades, the sight of Verrazano's *La Dauphine* may have been the first time that these Native Americans had laid eyes on an oceangoing sailing ship; they were understandably alarmed.

As the French sailors made their way inland, Verrazano reported:

> *By searching around we discovered in the grass a very old woman and young girl of about eighteen or twenty, who had concealed themselves for the same reason; the old woman carried two infants on her shoulders, and behind her neck a little boy eight years of age; when we came up to them they began to shriek and make signs to them who had fled to the woods.*

Verrazano offered the frightened Native Americans some food, which the old woman and the young boy accepted. The girl, however, threw the food on the ground. Her distrust of the European strangers was well founded. According to Verrazano:

> *We took the little boy from the old woman to carry with us to France, and would have taken the girl also, who was very beautiful and very tall, but it*

was impossible because of the loud shrieks she uttered as we attempted to lead her away having to pass some woods, and being far from the ship, we determined to leave her and take the boy only.

Having kidnapped a defenseless eight-year-old boy, Verrazano turned his attention to the hunting habits of the Native Americans: "They take birds and fish for food, using snares and bows of hard wood, with reeds for arrows, in the ends of which they put the bones of fish and other animals. The animals in these regions are wilder than in Europe from being continually molested by the hunters."

The Italian explorer was also interested in the dugout canoes used by the Native Americans: "To hollow out their boats they burn out as much of a log as is requisite, and also from the prow to the stern to make them float well on the sea." In addition, the Italian explorer remarked, "We also found wild roses, violets, lilies, and many sorts of plants and fragrant flowers different from our own."

Having completed smelling the roses, Verrazano ended his exploration of the Maryland mainland and led the landing party back to their ship. After sailing through the Sinepuxent Inlet, Verrazano continued northward. As he sailed past what is today the Ocean City beach, the Italian captain kept the

This parade float commemorated Verrazano's encounter with the Native Americans. *Courtesy of the Julia A. Purnell Museum.*

ship far enough from the beach to avoid the dangerous shoals off Fenwick Island. When he reached Cape Henlopen, he was so far from the coast that Verrazano failed to spot the entrance to Delaware Bay. He continued northward, where he entered the mouth of the Hudson River and explored the New England coast before the cautious explorer turned *La Dauphine* eastward and headed home.

Verrazano's inability to find a water passage to the East cooled European interest in North America. By keeping *La Dauphine* far from the beach, Verrazano avoided the fate that befell the *Santa Maria*; however, his caution caused him to miss several important geographic features along the coast. To commemorate his visit to the Hudson River, a large suspension bridge near New York City was named in his honor. To memorialize his visit to Maryland, a somewhat smaller bridge that connects the mainland to Assateague Island was named after Verrazano.

The cautious explorer met his demise a few years after visiting the Maryland coast, though the manner of Verrazano's death has been a matter of dispute. Some contend that he was killed by pirates, but others, including the eminent maritime historian Samuel Eliot Morison, believe that Verrazano met a violent end. In 1528, Verrazano was sailing in the West Indies, where he stopped near one of the islands and anchored a safe distance from the beach. As he had done along the Maryland coast, he decided to go ashore in a small boat. When he reached the beach, Verrazano was met by a group of island natives who seized him, built a fire, roasted and ate the first European tourist to visit the Ocean City area.

Following Verrazano's brief visit to the Ocean City area, two Spanish explorers, Estavan Gomez and Lucas Vasquez de Ayllon, sailed by the Maryland beach but failed to stop. The Spanish were far more interested in finding gold and silver in Central and South America than in spending a few hours enjoying the sun and surf. It was late in the sixteenth century before English colonists began to arrive in the mid-Atlantic region when several ships carrying colonists and supplies to the first English settlement on the Outer Banks of North Carolina passed along the Maryland coast. Vessels owned by Sir Walter Raleigh and commanded by Sir Francis Drake may have passed close to today's Ocean City beach, but these Englishmen failed to stop on the Maryland coast to savor the pleasures of a day lounging on the sand.

It was not until the seventeenth century that the next European explorer arrived in Worcester County. In 1608, Captain John Smith (of Pocahontas fame) left the Jamestown colony to explore the Chesapeake Bay and its tributaries. He sailed down the James River and across the bay to the mouth

Captain John Smith opened the way for European colonists to settle in the coastal region. *Courtesy of the Julia A. Purnell Museum.*

of the Pocomoke River. Smith continued up the river into Worcester County, but he apparently did not venture far from the river. He stopped short of the coastal bays and returned back down the Pocomoke River.

When Smith returned to England, he published a map of his travels. Much of Worcester County appears on Smith's map, which shows a serpentine route for the Pocomoke River. Unlike the cautious Verrazano, who assumed that the water that he saw west of the Outer Banks was the Pacific Ocean, Smith's map does not show areas that he did not see on the Maryland coast. On John Smith's map, the Atlantic shoreline is vaguely drawn, and much of the coast is obscured by an illustration of a cartographer's compass. The first colonists to arrive in the Ocean City area followed John Smith's route, and they traveled from the Chesapeake Bay and up the Pocomoke River. By the middle of the seventeenth century, there were a few villages scattered about Worcester County, but colonists avoided settling too close to the beach.

Accidental Tourists

In September 1649, Henry Norwood and more than three hundred passengers boarded the *Virginia Merchant* for the voyage from England to Jamestown, Virginia. Norwood wrote a detailed account of the trip that included a sobering depiction of an ocean voyage in the seventeenth century. As the *Virginia Merchant* crossed the Atlantic, the ship encountered several severe storms that delayed it from reaching the American mainland for several months, damaged the ship and drove the colonists to the edge of starvation.

Near the end of December, the *Virginia Merchant* reached the Ocean City coast. Like Verrazano, some of the sailors aboard the ship were very concerned that the *Virginia Merchant* would run afoul of a shoal; the captain anchored the ship a considerable distance from the surf. Norwood and some of the sick passengers piled into a small boat and rowed to the beach.

For the first time in months, the colonists were freed from the constant motion of the sea, and the uninhabited dunes of Fenwick Island provided firm beds for the Norwood party, who enjoyed a good night's sleep. The next morning, the colonists on the beach awoke to the startling sight of the *Virginia Merchant* under full sail. According to Norwood:

> *The first object we saw at sea was the ship under sail, standing for the capes with what canvass could be made to serve the turn. It was a very heavy prospect to us who remained (we knew not where) on shore, to see ourselves thus abandon'd by the ship…In this amazement and confusion of mind that no words can express, did our miserable distress'd party console with each other our being so cruelly abandon'd and left to the last despairs of human help, or indeed of ever seeing more the face of man.*

For reasons that have never been explained, the captain of the *Virginia Merchant* decided to continue the journey to Virginia. Norwood and his dozen companions were marooned. In the seventeenth century, one of the inlets was located a short distance north of the Maryland border, and a second inlet cut across the beach less than a mile south of the boundary. The Norwood party quickly discovered these two inlets that prevented them from traveling along the coast, but they failed to spot the marshy neck of land that connected Fenwick Island with the mainland.

The stranded colonists, who had only a few meager supplies, were plunged into despair. When the weather deteriorated, the stranded colonists had grave difficulty foraging for food. It was not long before many in Norwood's party were starving. He urged them to adopt a desperate measure to survive:

> *Of the three weak women before-mentioned, one had the envied happiness to die about this time; and it was my advice to the survivors, who were following her apace, to endeavor their own preservation by converting her dead carcass into food, as they did to good effect. The same counsel was embrac'd by those of our sex: the living fed upon the dead; four of our company having the happiness to end their miserable lives.*

As the colonists began to die, Norwood decided that the only possibility of salvation was

> *to attempt to cross the creek, and swim to the main (which was not above an hundred yards over) and being there to coast along the woods to the south- west (which was the bearing of Virginia) until should meet Indians, who would either relieve or destroy us.*

As he contemplated this last desperate attempt to reach safety, Norwood was busy tending a fire when he was startled by the approach of several Native Americans: "[I] discovered their faces with most cheerful smiles, without any kind of arms, or appearance of evil design; the whole number of them (perhaps twenty or thirty in all) consisting of men, women and children; all that could speak accosting us with joyful countenances, shaking hands with every one they met."

A short time later, the Native Americans loaded the surviving English settlers into dugout canoes and ferried them to the mainland. After they crossed the coastal bay, Norwood's party was led to a Native American village. Norwood described the accommodations that he was afforded:

> *I enjoyed in this poor man's cottage, which was made of nothing but mat and reeds, and bark of trees fix'd to poles. It had a loveliness and symmetry in the air of it, so pleasing to the eye, and refreshing to the mind, that neither the splendor of the Escorial, nor the glorious appearance of Versailles were able to stand in competition with it. We had a boiled swan for supper, which gave plentiful repast to all our upper mess. Our bodies thus refresh'd with meat and sleep, comforted with fires, and secured from all the changes and inclemencies of that sharp piercing cold season.*

After the colonists had recovered from their ordeal, the Native Americans helped the settlers make their way to Jamestown. It would be another half a century before European colonists would settle near the surf. In 1702, William Whittington took possession of a grant of one thousand acres on Assateague Island. Whittington dubbed his land "Baltimore's Gift," and he used the area for grazing livestock. It would be another century and a half before Ocean City would be established, but in the meantime, the coast would be visited by more menacing characters than the accidental tourists of Henry Norwood and his unfortunate party.

PIRATES, GENTLEMEN AND LADIES

Verrazano's cautious exploration and Norwood's unfortunate marooning did little to convince others to visit the desolate Maryland coast, but the pirate Blackbeard and other cutthroats found the uncharted inlets and quiet coastal bays rather inviting. Here was a place where the outlaw buccaneers could replenish their provisions and repair their ships without fear of capture. At the beginning of the eighteenth century, most of the settlers established farms along the Pocomoke River, and only a few law-abiding colonists joined Whittington on the barrier islands.

In 1699, Nathaniel Blackiston, the colonial governor of Maryland, received a report that the pirate William Kidd was sailing along the North American coast and that the notorious pirate might attempt to use the coastal bays of Maryland as a hideout. To meet this threat, Governor Blackiston determined to use his utmost "Care and Diligence to Apprehend Captain Kidd the pirate and his crew in case any of them should come into this province." The governor sent warrants to every county authorizing Kidd's arrest, but the pirate wisely bypassed the Maryland coast.

A few years after Blackiston sounded the alarm over a possible visit by Captain Kidd, Edward Teach landed without fanfare on Assateague Island. The fiery-eyed Teach was an imposing figure who usually armed himself with assorted dirks, knives, cutlasses and pistols. To impress his crew members, Teach liked to take several of his fellow pirates below deck, where he ignited pots of sulfur lightly laced with gunpowder. When the choking crew members scrambled out of the ship's hold, Teach remained behind, bellowing with laughter. To enhance his menacing appearance, Teach sometimes put short pieces of smoldering line into his hat so that his head was shrouded in a cloud of smoke. When he landed on Assateague

Island, however, Teach had a full dark beard that earned him his infamous nickname, "Blackbeard."

Popular legend has it that Blackbeard came to the coastal bays behind today's Ocean City to bury treasure. More likely Teach came to the calm waters behind the coastal island to repair his ship, take on provisions and visit his wife on Assateague Island. The small pine grove on Assateague that Blackbeard was said to have visited was home to one of at least a dozen wives whom Teach had scattered at various hideouts along the Atlantic coast.

Before he became a pirate, Blackbeard had been a common sailor of no particular standing, but some of his cohorts were different. Stede Bonnet was from a well-to-do English family, who had a successful sugar plantation on the island of Barbados in the West Indies. After serving in the British army, Bonnet was considered one of the leading men of Bridgetown, the capital of Barbados, before he enlisted a crew to go pirating with him. Bonnet's decision to become a pirate was a result of difficulties that he was having with his wife. Daniel Defoe delicately wrote in *A General History of the Pyrates* that Bonnet became a pirate because of "some discomforts he found in a married state."

Despite his lack of experience, Bonnet's career as a pirate began successfully. Sailing in a ship named *Revenge*, he captured several ships off the southern tip of Delmarva. After plundering those vessels of everything of value, Bonnet sailed northward, past Maryland, to Long Island, where he captured several more vessels. Sailing south, Bonnet arrived off South Carolina, where the gentleman pirate fell in with Blackbeard. Recognizing at once Bonnet's feeble knowledge of maritime matters, Blackbeard immediately placed one of his men in command of the *Revenge*. Forced to sail aboard Blackbeard's ship, it was reported that Bonnet walked the decks dressed in his "morning gown"; he spent most of his time reading books from the library that he had shipped aboard the *Revenge*.

While Blackbeard ran into some difficulties with his ship, Bonnet regained command of the *Revenge*, and he sailed northward and again cruised along the Maryland coast. After capturing a ship off Cape Henlopen, Bonnet headed south, but his luck ran out off North Carolina, where he was captured by the authorities. It is not known if Bonnet sailed into the coastal bays near today's Ocean City during any of his several trips along the Maryland coast.

Blackbeard and Bonnet were not the only buccaneers to sail the coastal waters near Ocean City. John Rackham, whose manners were as colorful as Bonnet's, is believed to have followed in Blackbeard's wake to Assateague Island. Unlike the brutish Blackbeard, Rackham was known as a gentleman who graciously allowed his captives to go free after he relieved them of their valuables. In addition to his civil manners, Rackham shunned the coarse clothing worn by most pirates. His fondness for fancy shirts, colorful waistcoats and bright breeches earned Rackham the nickname "Calico Jack." Some of Rackham's shipmates may not have been as well dressed as Calico Jack, but they were distinctive pirates in their own right.

Anne Bonny was still a rebellious teenager who had had several scrapes with the law when she met Calico Jack. The two fell in love, stole a sloop and began to raid ships along the Atlantic coast. Anne Bonny was not the only female in Rackham's pirate gang. Mary Read, who had disguised herself as a man and served in the Flemish army, also joined Calico Jack's crew. Aboard ship, Anne and Mary dressed in men's clothing, and they took an active part in Rackham's attacks on merchant ships. One of their victims later testified that they "wore men's jackets, and long trousers, and handkerchiefs tied about their heads; and that each of them had a machete and pistol in their hands, and cursed and swore at the men, to murder the deponent; and that they should kill her, to prevent her coming against them."

Calico Jack and Anne Bonny spent two years raiding ships in the busy coastal trade, preferring to use fast-sailing sloops that blended well with the vessels used along the coast. Rackham's sloop could easily navigate Sinepuxent Inlet and the other narrow channels that led to the calm waters of the coastal bays.

In 1720, the English decided to crack down on Rackham and other pirates operating along the Atlantic coast. In an effort to escape the British, Calico Jack and his two female shipmates sailed southward into the Caribbean Sea. Rackham encountered a privateer that had been commissioned to hunt and capture pirates. After the privateer fired a broadside into the sloop, Anne Bonny and Mary Read armed themselves with pistols and muskets. The two women cursed and screamed for the others to fight back, but Calico Jack and his crew meekly surrendered. Calico Jack Rackham was tried and convicted of being a pirate. Before he was executed, Rackham was allowed to visit Anne, who was awaiting her own trial. Anne gave her lover little comfort on his way to the gallows. She reportedly told him that "[i]f he had fought like a man, he need not have been hang'd like a dog." Anne Bonny and Mary Read were also found guilt of piracy and were sentenced to hang. After the sentence was announced, Anne and Mary announced that they were both pregnant; according to English custom, their sentences were commuted.

Sometime during the first half of the eighteenth century, the pirate Charles Wilson paid a quiet visit to the Worcester County coast. When Wilson turned to piracy in the 1730s, he followed in the wake of Captain Kidd and

Blackbeard. Wilson's career as a pirate had been a long one, but his exploits were not so spectacular as to attract much attention. Wilson's low profile enabled him to evade capture for many years, but he was eventually arrested and executed for piracy. Two hundred years after his death, a serendipitous discovery led treasure hunters to the Ocean City beach. As recounted by historians Reginald V. Truitt and Millard G. Les Callette, a letter was found in 1948 in the lid of an old trunk. The letter had been written by Wilson:

> *To my brother George, there are three creeks lying 100 paces or more north of the second inlet above the Chincoteague Island, Virginia, which is at the southward end of the Peninsula. At the head of the third creek to the northward is a bluff facing the Atlantic Ocean with cedar trees growing on it each about 1 1/3 yards apart. Between the trees I buried in ten ironbound chests, bars of silver, gold, diamonds and jewels to the sum of 200,000 pounds sterling. Go to "Woody Knoll" secretly and remove the treasure.*

Wilson's letter caused treasure hunters to drool at the prospect of uncovering chests stuffed with bars of silver, gold, diamonds and jewels in the sands of Assateague Island. No doubt many have scoured the length and breadth of the island in hope of discovering just one of Wilson's ironbound chests, but none has been found.

Charles Wilson was one of several lesser-known cutthroats to ply their trade in the Ocean City area. On November 1, 1746, five pirates used a small rowboat to reach a sloop anchored in Sinepuxent Bay. When the brigands slipped aboard the sailing craft, they were challenged by a sailor. The five men attacked the seaman with an old scythe. The unfortunate sailor was quickly subdued and thrown into the sloop's hold, where he died a short time later. The pirates next attacked the sloop's only other crewman. After they slashed the man's cheek, the buccaneers convinced the man to cooperate with them. The pirates raised the sloop's anchor and set sail for Sinepuxent Inlet, where they promptly ran aground. The five brigands were unable to refloat the sloop, and they loaded what valuables they could into a small boat and rowed away.

The next morning, the sailor who had his face slashed was able to signal a passing vessel for help. A short time later, the high sheriff of Worcester County gathered a posse of coastal residents who followed a trail of plundered vessels. A North Carolina vessel had been attacked by the five pirates, but the small sailing craft carried only a load of potatoes. The marauders captured a

This nineteenth-century map shows Sinepuxent Bay, south of Ocean City. *Courtesy of the Julia A. Purnell Museum.*

more valuable sloop that they used to pursue a larger oceangoing ship, which they were able to seize. The five cutthroats appeared to be on the verge of a career of piracy on the high seas, but an offshore wind prevented them from sailing through the inlet into the Atlantic Ocean. While the pirates were waiting for the wind to change, two of the men whom they had captured declared that they would like to join the buccaneers. The two men told the pirate band that there was a nearby place where they could secure fresh water. The pirates allowed the two to take a small boat and row ashore.

As soon as the two men were out of sight of the pirates, they sounded the alarm. The coastal residents launched a flotilla of small boats that descended on the pirate ship. When the outlaws spotted the approaching vessels, they opened fire. After a furious gun battle, the fighting ceased when the pirates ran out of ammunition. The brigands knew that the punishment for piracy was death, and they were determined to escape capture. All five of the outlaws dived into the bay, but four of the pirates were quickly plucked from the water. The fifth had been wounded in the gun battle and drowned. The four captured men were tried for piracy and executed.

Although the authorities eventually killed Blackbeard and swiftly executed others convicted of piracy, the stories of pirates lurking on the dark sands of the Maryland coast persisted for generations. As the years passed, a scattering of families made their homes on Assateague Island. At night with the sea breeze whipping across the dark sand, it was not hard to imagine a cutthroat buccaneer making his way through Sinepuxent Inlet. Even when Ocean City was established, and vacationers began to arrive on the coast, children of coastal families were careful to be home before dark so that pirates would not get them.

A GREYHOUND AND THE PONIES

Skeptics may doubt that pirates buried treasure on the Maryland coast, but there is no question that the sands of the Ocean City area have led to the demise of many ships. Strong storms occasionally erode sand on the resort's beach, uncovering the remains of some lost shipwreck. On undeveloped Assateague Island, the timbers of a ruined hulk rest mournfully in the dunes. By the middle of the eighteenth century, the population of the coastal area had begun to grow, and many residents kept a careful eye on the beach so that they would be the first to spot a ship in distress. On September 6, 1750, the Spanish frigate *Greyhound*, commanded by Captain Daniel Huony, grounded a short distance from the Assateague beach. The ship's crew was able to ferry several chests of silver to shore. They then muscled the treasure across Assateague Island to the coastal bay, where they loaded the silver into small boats for the trip across the bay to the mainland. By the time the chests had been transferred to wagons, the storm that had firmly mired the *Greyhound* in the Assateague sand had abated. The ship appeared to be in no

Shipwreck timbers from long-lost vessels still litter Assateague Island. *Photo by Michael Morgan.*

immediate danger, and the Spanish captain and crew set out for Snow Hill with the chests of silver.

The Spanish were able to reach Snow Hill without incident, but on the Maryland beach, a horde of beachcombers had descended on the *Greyhound*. They removed what cargo remained on the ship, and then the scavengers stripped the vessel of its tools, weapons, sails and rigging. They even tore up the decks for the timber. Huony complained to the Maryland authorities: "Her decks were cut up by the country people of both provinces, and that all she had in her (worth taking) was plundered and carried away by persons… took and carried away effects and stores to the value of a considerable sum." By the time that the Spanish returned, the *Greyhound* had been picked clean, and the remains of the vessel were left to settle in the Assateague sand.

Although nothing is mentioned in the surviving records of the *Greyhound* sinking, many people point to this shipwreck to explain the origin of the wild ponies that inhabit Assateague Island. Tradition holds that the horses swam ashore and were allowed to roam freely on the barrier island, where a diet of coarse grasses stunted the growth of their offspring.

In 1871, the noted travel writer Bayard Taylor arrived on Assateague Island and made a discovery:

The wild ponies of Assateague Island graze on the marsh grasses as they have done for centuries. *Photo by Michael Morgan.*

This is the breeding-place of a race of ponies, which run wild, feeding on the strong beach grass, except once a year, when they are herded, the colts banded with the owners' marks, and the mature animals sold. Those I saw were very handsome creatures, of a bright bay color, and about the size of a Mexican mustang.

Six years after Taylor's visit, the artist Howard Pyle visited Assateague Island. Pyle was beginning his career as an author, artist and historian, and his article in the April 1877 issue of *Scribner's Monthly* was one of the most detailed descriptions of the barrier islands before they were dominated by Ocean City:

Assateague beach—a narrow strip of land, composed of pine woods, salt marshes and sand flats—lies between it and the ocean, separated from it by a channel about half a mile in width. Midway upon this beach stands Assateague lighthouse—a first class light, and one of the finest on the coast. Between this beach or island upon the one side and the mainland on the other, in calm, sleep bay, lies lazy Chincoteague. There is but little agriculture; the inhabitants depend upon the sale of the ponies and upon fishing for the necessaries of life, and mere necessaries suffice them.

His depiction of Assateague Island was not much different from what a modern visitor encounters today: "Thick pine woods cover the island, in virgin growth, here and there opening into a glade of marshy flat, stretching off for a mile or more, called 'the meadows,' where one occasionally catches a glimpse of a herd of ponies, peacefully browsing at a distance."

Pyle recounted an English origin of the ponies:

> *How these ponies first came upon the island is not known except through vague tradition, for which the first setters came there early in the eighteenth century, they found the animals already roaming wild about the piney meadows. The tradition received from the Indians of the main-land was that a vessel laded with horses, sailing to one of the Elizabethan settlements of Virginia, was wrecked upon the southern point of the island, where the horses escaped…The horses, left to themselves upon their new territory, became entirely wild, and probably through hardships endured, degenerated into a peculiar breed of ponies.*

Pyle witnessed what has become an annual tradition: "Many of the ponies are taken over the narrow channel that separates Chincoteague from Assateague, to run wild upon the latter island, which is largely unclaimed land. We were so fortunate as to witness the lively scene of the swimming of a number of ponies across the channel or inlet."

Over the years, the traditional notion has persisted that the Assateague ponies descended from horses that survived a ship that foundered south of Ocean City. Several of the barrier islands along the Atlantic coast are home to similar herds of wild ponies, and some speculate that their ancestors may have been horses that farmers had let loose on the islands to graze. Whatever their origin, the Assateague ponies remain one of the principal attractions of the Ocean City area.

CHAPTER 2

WITH A BACKBONE
OF IRON

THE UNEVEN HAND OF ENGLISH JUSTICE

For most early residents of Worcester County, the area near the Great Cypress Swamp was to be avoided. When Edward Whaley arrived in the coastal region, the swamp covered more than fifty thousand acres that straddled the border between Maryland and Delaware. The swamp was a traceless wasteland of soggy ground and towering cypress trees inhabited by snakes, bears, brigands and others looking for a place to hide.

In the late seventeenth century, the English civil war pitted the forces of Parliament (led by Oliver Cromwell) against those of King Charles I. Cromwell's army defeated the king, who was captured and tried as a "[t]yrant, traitor, murderer, and a public and implacable enemy of the Commonwealth of England." Parliament found Charles guilty, and he was summarily beheaded. A decade later, royal power was restored when Charles II (son of the executed king) gained control of England. Charles II was determined to avenge the death of his father, and he began to hunt down all those who had signed the king's death warrant. Edward Whaley, who had supervised the imprisonment of Charles I, was among those who fled the wrath of Charles II.

Shortly after Whaley disappeared from England, a colonist named Edward Whaley settled in a secluded corner of Worcester County. The new colonist avoided public contact, and there were those who whispered that the recluse was the regicide himself. Over a century after Edward Whaley settled in the coastal region, one of his descendants, Peter Whaley, believed that it was time to exploit the resources of the Great Cypress Swamp.

Cypress is a durable wood that is nearly impervious to rot. In addition, the wood can be split easily into shingles. The logs best suited for making shingles came from trees that had fallen and lay impressed in the boggy bottom of the swamp. In the nineteenth century, Peter Whaley began to harvest the cypress from the swamp and split them into shingles. When enough shingles had been cut, he carted them eastward to a branch of the St. Martin River and then shipped through the Sinepuxent Inlet to buyers throughout the mid-Atlantic region. It is believed that some of the shingles cut in the eighteenth century still grace homes in Maryland, Delaware and elsewhere. Whether the Whaleys of Worcester County were descended from the man who had voted to execute the king of England has never been firmly established, but other residents of the Ocean City area were definitely descended from people who had experienced the uneven hand of English justice.

In the middle of the eighteenth century, England and France were locked in a titanic struggle over the control of North America that culminated in the French and Indian War. Nova Scotia had originally been settled by the French, but by 1713 the province had been ceded to the British. Although the British allowed their new subjects in Nova Scotia a great deal of independence, many English leaders believed that the Acadians remained loyal to France. When the French and Indian War began in 1755, the British feared that the Acadians would aid the French, and the English decided to relocate the population of Nova Scotia.

The French and Indian War had barely begun when Michel David and the other Acadian men were crowded into their small Nova Scotia church. David listened in silent disbelief as the words of the English official proclaimed that their world was at an end. The Acadians had been banished from their homes, and David would soon begin a dreary journey that would end in Worcester County.

On September 5, 1755, every Acadian male was summoned to gather at the local church. Michel David and the men crowded into the small church, where a detachment of British soldiers awaited them. At three o'clock in the afternoon, an officer began to read the king's proclamation: "Your lands and tenements and cattle and livestock of all kinds are forfeited to the crown, with all your other effects, except money and household goods, and that you yourselves are to be removed from this his province."

Although the men had been segregated from the women and children, the officer announced that they would be reunited with their families for the trip to their new homes. Despite the confiscation of all their goods (except those that they could carry) and the forced relocation, the officer hoped "[t]hat in whatever part of the world your lot may fall you may be faithful subjects and a peaceable and happy people."

After the proclamation had been read, the British soldiers, with fixed bayonets, herded the men to five transport ships. Next, the women and children were rounded up and brought to the ships. The English made an attempt to reunite families and to keep Acadians from the same village together, but in the confusion, some families were separated. Fortunately, Michel David was joined by his wife, Genevieve, and their children, Anne, Michel, Joseph and Paul, aboard the same ship. After the village had been evacuated, the English burned the town to the ground to discourage any hope that the Acadians could return home.

The ship carrying the David family sailed southward along the Atlantic coast until it turned into the Chesapeake Bay. When the ship reached Annapolis, the Maryland authorities decided to disperse the Acadians throughout the colony. The David family and about fifty other Acadians (including members of the Dechamp, Douliard, Forest, Granger, Leblanc, Lucas, Melanson and Tibodot families) were dispatched to Worcester County. At that time, the majority of the settlers in Worcester County were from England, but the county did have a number of settlers from France. The Aydolett, Devereaux, Perdue and Purnell families were well established in the coastal region when the Acadians arrived.

When the French and Indian War ended in 1763, conditions began to improve. The Acadians were allowed to return to Nova Scotia, but the David family decided to remain in Worcester County, where others were experiencing English justice.

The Times Are Dreadful, Dismal, Doleful, Dolorous and Dollar-Less

In 1763, the year the French and Indian War ended, the doors to St. Martin's Church were flung open for the first time. For many years, there had been so few settlers in this section of coastal Maryland that church service had been held in a temporary "chapel of ease" used by visiting clergymen. By the middle of the eighteenth century, northern Worcester County was finally attracting enough colonists to warrant the building of a permanent church.

Through much of the colonial period, tobacco was the main crop of Worcester County and Maryland, and it became the practice to reckon prices in terms of tobacco. No one carried a stack of tobacco leaves to the

The sturdy brick construction of St. Martin's Church has enabled it to withstand the ravages of time. *Photo by Michael Morgan.*

local general store to make a purchase, but receipts for tobacco stored in warehouses were often passed around as currency.

When the construction of St. Martin's was begun, the members of the church made an agreement with a local builder to construct a brick church with a

> *door in each side of the Church and one at the West end, seven windows made according to a plan that Mr. Robert Kirby drew, the windows to be glass in with Single Crown or good northward Glass to be raised with leads and Pulleys, folding doors…the said doors and Windows to be primed with Linseed Oil and Red Oker and to be done over a second time with a lead Color.*

While the church was being built, the plans were changed. The building was enlarged by ten feet, and by the time it was completed, St. Martin's cost 103,000 pounds of tobacco to build the solid brick structure roofed with heavy cedar shingles that were two feet long and one inch thick. The interior walls of the new church were plastered and whitewashed. The

The oak pews, gallery and pulpit helped finish off the interior of St. Martin's Church. *Photo by Michael Morgan.*

solid white of the walls was relieved by oak wainscoting of the gallery built over the entrance.

Shortly after St. Martin's was finished, residents of Worcester County who picked up the October 31, 1765 issue of the *Maryland Gazette* (the only Maryland newspaper available at that time) were greeted by the crude image of the skull and crossbones. Pirates had not invaded the coastal area, but rather the British Parliament had passed the Stamp Act, and most of Maryland was in an uproar. According to the *Maryland Gazette*, the Stamp Act was an act of piracy, and the image of the skull and crossbones was accompanied by the ominous assessment: "The times are DREADFUL, DISMAL, DOELFUL, DOLORUS AND DOLLAR-LESS."

The passage of the Stamp Act struck a vital nerve in most coastal colonists, who considered themselves as English people living in America, and they clung to the belief that only their own representatives could tax them. Not a single American colonist sat in the British Parliament, and residents of Worcester County felt that taxes passed by Parliament violated their rights as Englishmen.

The American outcry over the loathsome tax caused the British Parliament to repeal the Stamp Act, but several years of continued boisterous protests over tea, taxes and the rights of colonists eventually precipitated the

American Revolution. In April 1775, fighting erupted between the colonists and the British at the Battle of Lexington and Concord. Many men from Worcester County enlisted in the Continental forces, and they marched to Massachusetts, where they joined General George Washington's army. Other county residents joined the Sinepuxent, Snow Hill and Wicomico militia battalions to fight the British.

Although many coastal residents supported the war against Great Britain, there was also a large number of people in Worcester County who remained loyal to the king. After the fighting started, the Tories were nearly as quick to organize as the Patriots were. In November 1775, a committee of Worcester Patriots wrote to state authorities: "We and the rest of the friends of liberty in this country are in a bad situation; we have no ammunition and the Tories exceed our number. We hope you will send us assistance as soon as you can."

By 1776, only a few primitive buildings had been erected on the entire length of the Maryland beach that would one day be home to Ocean City. Some farmers used the sandy islands to graze livestock; other residents occasionally walked the beaches to hunt for salvageable shipwreck debris. American vessels attempting to avoid ships of the British navy sometimes slipped into Sinepuxent Inlet, but the waterway was so narrow that ships sometimes had difficulty navigating through it.

In March, 1777, the privateer brig *General Mifflin* was sailing along the coast when it was overtaken by a storm. The captain decided to run into Sinepuxent Inlet and ride out the storm in the protected coastal bay. According to the *Pennsylvania Gazette*:

> *On the sixth instant, the privateer brig General Mifflin, Captain Hamilton, of this port returning from a cruise was overtaken by a violent storm, which determined the Captain to carry her into Sinepuxent, but the pilot, being ignorant of the channel, unfortunately ran her on shore where the vessel bilged, and was soon filled with water. The hands (ninety odd) were on the quarter deck the whole night, and suffered exceedingly and in the morning go on shore on a desolate beach, covered with snow where seventeen perished, but by timely assistance the remainder of the crew were saved. Near three thousand pounds worth of prize effect were on board, which were lost with the vessel.*

In spite of these difficulties, Patriot vessels continued to sail close to shore to avoid capture by the British navy, and they usually sailed safely past the deserted Maryland beach. In 1777, a ship carrying the family of one of America's greatest naval heroes quietly made its way along the coast and into Sinepuxent Inlet.

How Stephen Decatur's parents reached Berlin during the American Revolution is a matter of conjecture. Bad roads made overland travel difficult, and most long trips were conducted via water. The Decatur family lived in Philadelphia, where American independence had been proclaimed in 1776. Stephen's father was an ardent Patriot, and he was an officer in the Continental navy. In September 1777, the British advanced toward Philadelphia, and the Decatur family fled the city. They may have traveled overland, but in all likelihood, the Decaturs boarded a small vessel, sailed down the Delaware Bay to the Atlantic Ocean and headed southward along the coast until they reached the Sinepuxent Inlet. It would have been natural for the Decatur family to use the inlet to reach the town of Sinepuxent, which is now Berlin, where on January 5, 1779, Stephen Decatur was born.

Decatur was still a youngster when the American Revolution ended and the Continental navy was disbanded. When he was a teenager, however, attacks on American merchant ships by north African pirates led to the creation of the United States Navy. Stephen Decatur was twenty years old when he entered the navy as a midshipman and began his meteoric rise to fame. During the war against the pirates of north Africa, Decatur led a small party of sailors who slipped into the harbor of Tripoli, where they burned

A portion of the house in which Stephen Decatur was born near Berlin survived for a century after his birth. *Courtesy of the Julia A. Purnell Museum.*

the captured American frigate *Philadelphia*. Admiral Horatio Nelson called Decatur's feat "the most bold and daring act of the age."

Decatur won not only victories but also the universal respect of the men he led. A marine who served under the Worcester County native wrote, "The intrepid Decatur is as proverbial among sailors, for the good treatment of his men, as he is for his valor. Not a tar, who ever sailed with Decatur, but would almost sacrifice his life for him."

After fighting with distinction during the War of 1812, Decatur was appointed one of the three commissioners who oversaw the administration of the navy. In addition to his naval career, Decatur was applauded for his stirring toast: "Our country! In her intercourse with foreign nations may she always be in the right; but our country, right or wrong!"

Stephen Decatur may have had but a single fault: fighting duels. By the early nineteenth century, dueling had developed an elaborate set of rules that dealt with challenges, seconds and the satisfaction of honor. In Decatur's time, many countries had outlawed dueling, but the custom remained popular with young military officers. In 1804, there was a strong outcry against the medieval custom when Vice President Aaron Burr killed Alexander Hamilton in a duel, but this did not dissuade Decatur from dueling.

A modest stone monument sits in a park on the edge of Berlin to mark the spot where Stephen Decatur was born. *Photo by Michael Morgan.*

Decatur was an expert shot, and he did not shy from any challenge. In 1802, Decatur offered to fight a duel for his friend, William Bainbridge. On another occasion, he was to fight a duel with a man whom, Decatur believed, was a poor shot. Before this duel, Decatur told one of his friends that there was no need to kill this man and that he intended to shoot the man only in the hip. Decatur emerged from this duel unscathed, and his poorly shooting opponent suffered the predicted hip wound.

In 1820, Decatur was forty-one years old and at the height of his fame, but he was also engaged in a long-running dispute with a former naval officer, James Barron. Decatur and Barron decided to meet on the traditional dueling grounds outside Washington near Bladensburg, Maryland. After the two men fired, Stephen Decatur fell, mortally wounded.

The modest house in which Stephen Decatur was born survived for over a century after his birth before it was torn down. Today, a pleasant park and a small marker indicate the place in Berlin where the fugitive Decatur family lived during the American Revolution. A dozen miles up the road from Decatur's birthplace, the solidly built St. Martin's Church still sits in a grove of shady trees. Both sites are quiet and peaceful and belie the times that were so dreadful, dismal, doleful, dolorous and dollar-less.

THE ENTAILED HAT

For Joseph G. Widener, the ruddy color of Nassawango Creek could mean only one thing, and in 1788, he decided that the creek would make him rich. When Maryland was an English colony, British laws discouraged the establishment of manufacturing in America. After the American Revolution, though, the way was open for entrepreneurs like Widener to make their fortunes.

Widener believed that the rusty color of Nassawango Creek was caused by deposits of iron that lined the banks of the waterway, and he decided to establish a furnace to turn the bog iron into nails, hinges, horseshoes, buckles and other iron products needed by the growing American population. Widener had a great idea, but he was unprepared for the complexity of early ironworking. The mining of bog iron along Nassawango Creek could be done from the surface, but all of the work had to be done by hand. In addition, the only way to produce a fire hot enough to melt the iron ore was by the use of charcoal. At that time, charcoal did not come in neat little briquettes familiar to backyard chefs. Charcoal in the late eighteenth century was wood that had the moisture charred out of it.

Two men tend an earth-covered stack of simmering charcoal. *Courtesy of the Delaware Public Archives.*

The forests of Worcester County that surrounded the Nassawango Furnace had enough timber to supply the needs of the furnace, but the wood had to be reduced to charcoal. Once the trees had been felled and the wood cut into convenient lengths, the timber was carefully stacked in a conical pile. After the timber stack was covered with a layer of mud, the collier ignited the wood, which smoldered for several days as the moisture in the timber was consumed.

To operate his ironworks, Widener used a labor force that included a number of slaves, one of whom was Sampson Harmon, born in 1790. The manufacture of iron required a labor force with a wide range of skills. Forge men, hammer men, blacksmiths, colliers and others possessed skills that were difficult to acquire. In order to keep their skilled slaves from running away, many owners often allowed them to keep any income that they generated from outside work, and some slaves were able to buy their freedom. Many of the skilled slaves continued working at the furnace even as freemen. This was the case with Harmon, who became a freeman and continued to be employed at the ironworks.

After just a few years, Widener abandoned his ironworking efforts; by 1829, his holdings passed into the hands of the Maryland Iron Company, which acquired five thousand acres of land west of Snow Hill. A tall brick furnace was built, and a thriving village known as Furnace Town developed along the banks of Nassawango Creek. In 1837, Furnace Town was taken over by Thomas A. Spence, and Sampson Harmon became his personal servant.

For more than a decade, the smoky plume of Spence's ironworks drifted over coastal Worcester County. While Thomas Spence prospered, a relative, Ara Spence, acquired a tract of land to the east on the banks of Chincoteague Bay. In addition to shipping farm produce, Spence shipped shingles and lumber from the landing on his estate through the inlet to markets along the East Coast. Some of Spence's neighbors used his pier to ship their goods, and the spot became known as "Spence's Landing." The ironmaster, Spence, joined his relatives at the landing and built a large house that overlooked Chincoteague Bay. The house gave a clear view of the activity at the landing, and the two-story mansion house enabled Spence to see across the coastal bay, over the barrier island and to the Atlantic. Apparently, Spence was so fond of this vista that he named his estate Ocean View. Spence's Landing became a popular place for the general public to picnic and enjoy the bay waters, and it eventually became known as "Public Landing."

By 1850, coal-fired blast furnaces located in the Appalachian Mountains

The Nassawango ironworks were abandoned in the nineteenth century, and for years the crumbling brick furnace was a reminder of the early industrialization of the coastal area. *Courtesy of the Julia A. Purnell Museum.*

began producing iron far more economically than the Nassawango Furnace, and Spence was forced to close the ironworks. Spence sold the village and left Furnace Town. When he died, his will stipulated: "I give to Ephraim K. Wilson of Worcester County all my negro slaves in trust that the said Ephraim K. Wilson shall as soon as possible after my death transfer said negroes to Liberia in Africa under the care of the Maryland State Colonization Society or the American Colonization Society as to him may seem best." His servant, Harmon, who had apparently earned his freedom and was not affected by Spence's will, decided to stay in the area. Harmon moved into a small cabin in the woods near Snow Hill, where he lived with a large black cat named "Tom."

While Harmon lived quietly in his cabin, far from public view, George Alfred Townsend was one of the most prominent American newspaper correspondents. Born in southern Delaware in 1841, Townsend's vivid dispatches during the Civil War garnered him a national audience. Following the war, he wrote a popular newspaper column under the nom de plume "Gath" that further enhanced his reputation. In addition, the Sussex County native also wrote a biography of Abraham Lincoln, numerous poems and several novels.

Townsend was in the Worcester County Courthouse in Snow Hill researching his mother's ancestors when he stumbled on a will in which a man left his son "my best hat…and no more of my estate." The unusual bequest sparked Townsend's creative instincts, and he set to work on the novel that he entitled *The Entailed Hat*, which became Townsend's most famous fictional work. *The Entailed Hat* was set in Maryland and southern Delaware during the early nineteenth century, and it vividly described the Nassawango ironworks, slavery and the notorious Patty Cannon, a serial killer, thief and kidnapper. One of the book's principal characters was the freeman Sampson Hat.

The Entailed Hat was fiction, but it was firmly grounded in historical fact. The novel took its title from one of the principal characters, Meschach Milburn, who insisted on wearing a large out-of-fashion hat that he had inherited. Sampson, Milburn's servant, looked after the headpiece, and he became known as Sampson Hat. When *The Entailed Hat* was published, many coastal residents recognized Sampson Harmon as the model for the character in Townsend's book, and they began calling him by the character's name.

The Entailed Hat has enjoyed enduring popularity, and the novel is still read today. Townsend's book brought Harmon an added degree of notoriety, but as the decades continued to pass, he could no longer live alone in the forests of Worcester County. Harmon eventually moved to the Worcester County Poor House Farm, where the remarkable man who experienced the rise and fall of the ironworking along Nassawango Creek lived out the last years of his life.

By the time Sampson Harmon died in 1898, Ocean City had begun its rise as a premier seaside resort. Although most visitors from Baltimore and Washington preferred to vacation in Ocean City, many Worcester County residents enjoyed spending a relaxing day at Spence's Landing, which had been renamed Public Landing. The waters of Chincoteague Bay were familiar, calm and teeming with fish, crabs and other wildlife. For those who wished to visit the ocean, the old Civil War sloop *Fairfield* ferried people across the bay to Assateague Island. A pier extended into the bay, and a short boardwalk lined the shore. Other amusements included a bathhouse, shooting gallery and a merry-go-round. A visitor to Public Landing recalled that "[t]here was a pier running out in the water; and it was at the end of the pier where boats came by…[there was a pavilion] where you could sit and eat lunch and all the stuff you want. And we went bathin' and crabbin' and oysterin' [and] clammin' there. It was a big place for that."

DeGulibert's Hotel provided accommodations for those who wished to stay at Public Landing for several days, but most visitors were residents of the coastal region who spent a day picnicking, fishing and crabbing. Public Landing usually did not attract large crowds, but on Foresters' Day, the first Thursday in August, the beach was packed with people. Foresters were people from the heavily wooded areas of Worcester County, and it became popular for the foresters to congregate at Public Landing. On Foresters' Day, families would arrive at Public Landing with baskets of fried chicken, baked treats and other goodies. Families staked out spots where they spread blankets on the ground for their picnic. Extra boats at the pier provided short rides on the bay for a dime. The tradition of Foresters' Day continued into the twentieth century, when it became known as Farmers' Day.

TO DEFEND THE UNION

At the end of October 1861, President Abraham Lincoln and the other members of the Union high command had a serious problem with Worcester County. Maryland was a slave state, and in the election of 1860, most Worcester County residents had voted for the Southern Democratic candidate John Breckinridge, who was an ardent defender of slavery. At the start of the Civil War, Worcester County held a pivotal position among the slaveholding areas on the Delmarva Peninsula. Sandwiched between Virginia (which had seceded from the Union) and Delaware (also a slave state), the Northern authorities believed that Southern sympathizers might rally the support of slaveholders to take control of the entire Eastern Shore. In addition, small vessels used Sinepuxent Inlet to carry on a lively coastal trade with secessionist Virginia.

Not all residents of Worcester County supported the South. After the firing on Fort Sumter, William Henry Purnell organized a military unit that he dubbed the "Purnell Legion"; it was composed of an infantry regiment, two companies of cavalry and two artillery batteries. The infantry regiment included an entire company of men who had been recruited in Worcester County.

With a local election scheduled for the first week in November, the Union authorities were afraid that the secessionists would use this election to gain control of the coastal area. On November 4, 1861, Colonel H.E. Paine of the Fourth Regiment of Wisconsin Volunteers commanded a force of Union troops that included the Purnell Legion. Paine was ordered to march to Snow Hill to quell Confederate activity in the coastal region. In addition, Paine was to prevent anyone from Accomac and Northhampton Counties in Virginia from attempting to vote in Maryland elections. Paine rounded up a number of suspected Confederate sympathizers, and among those arrested by the Union troops was state senator Teagle Townsend, whose house near Snow Hill was reputed to be a haven for those traveling south to join the Confederate army. Townsend was a member of the Maryland General Assembly, and he was a public advocate of secession. In addition, James Aydolette (who represented Worcester County in the Maryland House of Delegates) was also taken into custody.

The soldiers of the invading Federal army used restraint—there was little disruption of the civil population, and the election was conducted peacefully. Southern sympathizers from Virginia were unable to vote, and Worcester County remained firmly in the Union. After the initial threat to the Union in Maryland had been thwarted, Purnell grew tired of military life. He resigned from the Purnell Legion.

The resolute Union action in the coastal region not only secured the area for the Northern cause, but it also led to an unexpected supply of troops. When President Lincoln issued the Emancipation Proclamation, the nature of the struggle changed. When Lincoln proclaimed that all of the slaves in the rebelling states were free, the Civil War shifted from a conflict over states' rights to a crusade to end slavery. Newly freed men, who had not been viewed by most Northerners as potential troops, were now actively recruited for the Union army.

In Maryland, which remained loyal to the Union, slaves were not affected by the Emancipation Proclamation, but when the army recruiters arrived in

Worcester County in November 1863, Sarah Bruff decided to allow several of her slaves, including Isaiah Fassett, to enter the army. Fassett was born on March 17, 1844, to Andrew Fassett and Mary Bratten near Berlin. His mother was a slave and worked for Bruff, who also owned Isaiah's three brothers: Andrew, John and George. As a youngster, Isaiah had worked on Bruff's farm, where he also acquired some carpentry skills. When the army recruiters arrived, Bruff agreed to grant the Fassett brothers their freedom in return for $1,600 to compensate for her loss.

On the same day that they were freed, the Fassett brothers enlisted in the Ninth Regiment of United States Colored Troops. Isaiah was assigned to Company D, and after training at Benedict, Maryland, for several months, Fassett and the rest of the regiment were sent to the islands off the South Carolina coast, where they fought in several minor skirmishes. In August 1864, Fassett and the other troops of the Ninth Regiment were transferred to Virginia, where they became part of the Union forces that were besieging Richmond and Petersburg. The Ninth fought in the Battle of Fussel's Mills and participated in the unsuccessful assault on Fort Gilmore near Richmond.

In April 1865, the Confederate defense of Richmond collapsed. As General Robert E. Lee retreated toward Appomattox, Fassett's unit was one of the first Union regiments to enter the Confederate capital. As Fassett marched through the city, the Northern troops were cheered by throngs of former slaves. A week later, Lee surrendered and the Civil War came to an end.

Fassett's service with the Union army, however, was not over. The Ninth Regiment was sent to Brownsville, Texas, where Fassett spent a year on the American southern frontier. The Worcester County native was finally discharged from the army in November 1866.

After the Civil War, Fassett returned to the coastal region, where he married Sallie Purnell, and together they had eight children. To support his family, Fassett worked as a carpenter and built several houses in the coastal region. During these years, Fassett was an active member of the Grand Army of the Republic, an organization of veterans of the Union army. For many years, Fassett served as the commander of the Berlin post of the GAR.

In the late nineteenth and early twentieth centuries, the GAR sponsored commemorations of important Civil War battles. In 1913, a large contingent of veterans gathered at Gettysburg to mark the fiftieth anniversary of the Civil War's largest battle. At that time, many of the veterans vowed to reconvene on the battle's seventy-fifth anniversary. By 1938, Fassett, who was known as "Uncle Zear" and who had become a permanent fixture at Memorial Day parades in Berlin, was determined to attend the Gettysburg

The marker over Isaiah Fassett's grave in the black section of a cemetery near Berlin. *Photo by Michael Morgan.*

gathering. When he journey to Pennsylvania in 1938, Fassett was ninety-four years old, which was close to the average age of the 1,845 Civil War veterans who attended the gathering. The Union and Confederate survivors at Gettysburg were addressed by President Franklin Roosevelt, who said, "All of them we honor, not asking under which flag they fought—thankful that they stand together under one flag now."

Isaiah Fassett was born a slave, fought for the Union and his freedom and worked to remind people of the sacrifices that the troops, white and black, had made to put down the Southern rebellion. Reverend David Briddell has done groundbreaking research on Fassett and has identified 647 African Americans from Worcester County who served in the Union army. Briddell wrote:

> We do know that a significant portion of the Worcester County's white male population employed various strategies to evade being drafted or to render themselves exempt. Many other whites fled south to fight with the Confederate Army. Thus, it appears that it was the African-American soldiers who bore the brunt of Worcester County's participation in the military actions of the United States Government to abolish slavery and preserve a nation united, rather than divided.

When Fassett died in June 1946, he was the next to the last of Maryland's Civil War veterans. Fassett lies buried in a segregated cemetery outside Berlin.

CHAPTER 3

A SORT OF PARADISE

THE LADIES' RESORT TO THE OCEAN

When the Civil War ended in 1865, the Maryland seacoast was practically deserted. Periodically, beachcombers would appear on the sand in search of something valuable, and there were also occasional picnickers from the mainland who spent a day hunting bird eggs in the grassy areas just west of the dunes. Most residents of the mainland avoided the barrier island, which was used principally as a grazing area for livestock.

The Civil War sparked American industrial growth, promoted the development of a nationwide railroad system and taught many people the value of a few weeks' vacation. At the end of the war, Americans got back to peacetime pursuits, and some of them went to the beach. The well-to-do made Newport, Rhode Island, the premier seaside resort, and other locations along the coast scrambled to imitate it. Ocean City, however, was slow to get into the game. Bayard Taylor, the travel writer who had written a brief description of the Assateague ponies, visited the Maryland coast in 1871 and described the beach in glowing terms for *Harper's Monthly*:

> *The beach, a quarter of a mile in breadth, rises but a few feet above the sea level. There are some sheds for bathers and excursionists, facing the Atlantic, which here, growing gray in the sunset, rolled in, and broke in long, heavy, lazy swells. It was too tempting: a look at the sand assured us that the sea-nettles were unknown, and we presently meet the great, lifting masses of water, and rode them as if they were tame elephants.*

Taylor had traveled extensively, and he was able to compare the Maryland beach with others that he had visited:

> *Of all coast bathing this is the finest I ever saw. The sand, which like velvet to the feet, has a gradual slope; there is no perceptible under-tow or side current; and the lazy force of the huge waves, which subside rather than break violently, allows the bather to rock and swing upon them with a new sense of luxury, The temperature of the sea was perfect, and nothing but the falling twilight called us back to the shore.*

Although Taylor failed to describe any accommodations on the beach, by 1869 Isaac Coffin had opened the Rhode Island Inn, a modest establishment with spartan accommodations. Tradition has it that Coffin named the hotel "Rhode Island" because he had found a trailboard from a shipwreck with that name floating in the surf. When Isaac Coffin decided to build a small inn on the Maryland coast, he selected a deserted stretch of the beach where the mainland jutted toward the barrier island. The bulge in the mainland reduced the northern end of Sinepuxent Bay to a narrow waterway that was only a few hundred yards wide, and visitors to Coffin's Rhode Island Inn could be quickly ferried across the bay.

The Rhode Island Inn was not far from the surf, but most of Coffin's early guests had little interest in the beach. Many of the lodgers were sportsmen who were attracted by the large number of birds that frequented the coast. Unlike the devotees of the surf who appeared on the coast during the warm summer months, hunters arrived at Coffin's Rhode Island Inn during the colder months, when the migratory birds were prevalent along the coast. A reporter for the *New York Times* was enthralled with the beauty of the Maryland coast:

> *Of Synapuxant Beach much can be said in praise of its beauty, if beauty can be found in an unbroken line of fifty miles of sand-beach. Here and there occasionally heavy seas break over the beach and wash inlet to the bay, but the same storm which opens the inlet also closes it, so it is possible to drive with a horse and carriage from the Delaware line to Synapuxant Inlet, a distance of fifty miles.*

The reporter found that the Maryland beach was an island of sand that was unique from others along the Atlantic coast:

Often times not more than a few hundred feet wide, it never reaches a width of a mile and half. On one side is the great ocean, and on the other a shallow bay, the water of which is almost always tranquil, and is the natural home of the wild duck and wild goose, while oysters of the very best quality are found in it in great abundance. The bay is in some places ten miles wide. In others it narrows down to two hundred yards, and is from two to five feet deep.

With no humans to disturb them, wildfowl had been nesting in the coastal bays for centuries. In addition, the area was a convenient stopping point for thousands of migratory birds; during some times of the year, birds covered the surface of Sinepuxent Bay:

It is no uncommon sight to see acres of water literally alive with wild fowl. Here in this bay are to be found almost all the varieties of the wild duck known to the American hunter. The canvas-back duck and the mallard, the black duck and brent, the sprig and the teal, all feed and breed here; and in fact, the bays lying to the west of the Synapuxant Beach may really be called the home of the wild duck.

The reporter was less enthusiastic about the facilities available for humans along the coast:

The accommodations for gunners cannot be described as luxurious; and if a gunner from the city comes to this bay expecting to find hot and cold water in his room and gas-light furnished him, he will fare sadly. But if he comes expecting to find no accommodation, he may fare better, as occasionally there are to be found places along the shore where very good accommodations can be had, at liberal prices.

The sportsmen who hunted for wildfowl along the Maryland coast endured harsh conditions in the quest for their prey. After arising in the middle of the night, the hunters trekked across the dunes to a suitable location near the coastal bay frequented by the wildfowl. Some gunners dug holes in the sand; others hid behind a blind, waist-deep in water. In either case, a string of decoys was deployed to entice the passing birds to come within range.

A successful hunt often meant suffering attacks by mosquitoes, sand flies and other pesky residents of the coast. In addition, the gentlemen-sportsmen sometimes endured hours half-submerged in bone-chilling water. After

A large group of Ocean City bathers take their first tentative steps toward the surf. *Courtesy of the Julia A. Purnell Museum.*

the day's hunt was completed, the game was gathered together, and the sportsmen retraced their steps to the Rhode Island Inn, where the men spent the evening in the common sitting room smoking their pipes and discussing guns, decoys and the habits of various birds.

Isaac Coffin's Rhode Island Inn sat alone on the Maryland beach until 1872, when James Massey of Berlin opened an inn not far from Coffin's establishment. Coffin's and Massey's hotels sat on that part of the beach where the mainland jutted toward the barrier island and where Sinepuxent Bay was reduced to a channel a few hundred years wide. Although it was connected to Sinepuxent Bay, the water north of this narrow opening became known as the Isle of Wight Bay, which abutted Assawoman Bay. With the establishment of the first two hotels on the beach, the Maryland coast seemed ripe for development, and about this time, Stephen Taber arrived in Worcester County. As far as it is known, Taber spent very little time on the beach. It is probable that he never once took a dip in the surf or spent an afternoon enjoying the sun and sand. Despite spending so little time on the coast, Taber managed to make the first fortune in Ocean City.

In the years immediately following the Civil War, Taber began to buy up large chunks of coastal real estate until he had assembled a collection of coastal land that included one thousand acres on Assateague Island, which at that time was a continuous ribbon of sand along the Maryland coast. It has been estimated that Taber paid about fifteen dollars for each acre of land that he purchased on the mainland. On the other hand, the Taber's oceanfront property cost him only an average of ninety cents an acre.

Taber was not haphazard in his purchases of Worcester County real estate. He went out of his way to buy a single acre of land that was on the best route for a possible railroad line from Berlin to Ocean City. At the time that Tabor began his purchases, the railroad between Salisbury and Berlin had not yet been completed. Vacationers heading for the ocean had to travel over a dirt road to the west shore of Sinepuxent Bay, where they boarded a small boat and were ferried over to the barrier island.

With his land acquisitions in place, Taber called a meeting of interested investors at the new railroad depot in Berlin. The investors were eager to develop the Maryland beach, and Taber agreed to sell ten acres of oceanfront land to the investors for the hotel. Taber also agreed to throw in an option for fifty more acres of land that would be developed as town lots if the hotel proved successful. As plans for the hotel moved forward, the developers decided on a name of their new community. Perhaps in an effort to distinguish it from the rugged accommodations available to hunters, the new development was named the Ladies' Resort to the Ocean. Within a short time, however, the new resort would be known as Ocean City.

On July 4, 1875, several hundred people were ferried across the coastal bay to see the new Atlantic Hotel, which was receiving its finishing touches when the crowd arrived. According to a reporter from Salisbury, "The carpenters' hammer and saw is still heard all around the premises, and it will not be complete in all its surroundings for several days yet, but for the accommodation of two or three hundred guests they are well prepared, and when all is completed the can accommodate from 700 to 1000 guests." Ocean City had become a reality.

The new hotel featured an excellent orchestra, a fine restaurant and an unobstructed view of the beach. The reporter from Salisbury commented that "[t]he hotel is a marvel in architectural beauty and excellence rivaling the finest hotel on the Atlantic coast. The rooms are large and airy with the best ventilation one ever saw. The furniture is of the best quality, and surpasses anything in the line of bedding we have seen anywhere in a public house."

Soon, the Atlantic Hotel was joined by several other establishments, and Massey's hotel was renamed the Seaside; it was enlarged to include a "[f]irst-class bar, bowling alley and livery stable." Although the Seaside would be a landmark for many years, a street passed between it and the Atlantic

Hotel and, more importantly, the beach. It was not long before Ocean City's small cluster of buildings was well on its way to becoming a first-class resort. However, not all of the early reports of the town were positive. A year after the Atlantic Hotel opened, a reporter from Washington, D.C., complained:

> *Why the place from which I write should be called Ocean City, is to me an unexplained mystery. The name is certainly a misnomer. Before reaching here I anticipated seeing a town with depots, omnibuses, possibly horse-cars, and other appurtenances of a flourishing seaside resort, but upon arrival I was wholly mistaken. The place might, with great propriety, be called Atlantic Hotel, for it is only that and nothing more.*

A short time after the Atlantic Hotel was opened, a railroad trestle was built across Sinepuxent Bay, and the train was able to roll directly into Ocean City. An 1877 map of the resort shows the railroad track crossing the bay and swinging northward up Baltimore Avenue to the back entrance of the Atlantic Hotel. The map shows that the resort had been neatly divided into more than two hundred lots, but most of these were empty.

Three years after the Atlantic Hotel opened, the United States Life-Saving Service opened a station on the beach. Founded after the Civil War, the service was dedicated to assisting ships of sailors in distress. During the late nineteenth and early twentieth centuries, a series of stations was built along the coast. The Ocean City station was eventually joined by the Isle of Wight station to the north and stations at North Beach and Green Run Inlet to the south. In 1884, a visitor to the beach commented in the *New York Times*:

> *A stroll of three miles along the ocean shore…reveals the wonderfully destructive force of storms along this coast. Within that three miles we passed the wrecks of six fine vessels, of which have been cast ashore within two years. Besides these wrecks the remains of many others are to be seen… Our party gathered up enough Cumberland coal to do our cooking for a week or more, and there will be enough of this coal on the beach to supply a family with fuel for several years to come, as two large schooners laden with it were wrecked on the outer bar last year, and the ocean is continually washing it up on the beach.*

In addition to their normal duties, the surfmen provided a variety of other services. In the early twentieth century, the *Annual Report of the Life-Saving Service* summarized the diverse actions performed by the service's surfmen:

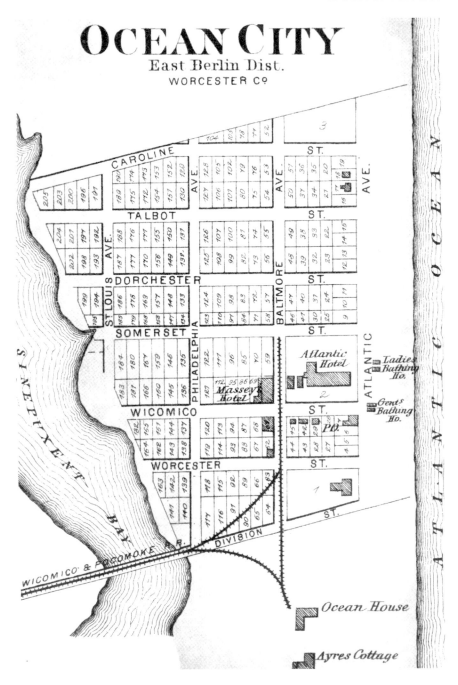

This nineteenth-century map shows the railroad trestle across Sinepuxent Bay, the Atlantic Hotel and separate bathhouses for men and women on the beach. *Courtesy of the Julia A. Purnell Museum.*

During the year 110 persons were saved from various situations of danger having no connection with disasters to boats or shipping. Thirty-three of these were imperiled bathers and swimmers; 20 had accidently fallen from piers, etc.; 47 were entrapped on breakwaters, rocks, trestles, and other exposed places by rising ides, rough seas, and floods; 2 (small boys) were adrift, one on a raft, the other in a rowboat; 2 had climbed 100 feet up the face of a cliff and were unable to get down; 1 had tried to commit suicide by jumping from a wharf; 1, an intoxicated man, was about to fall off a dock; 1 had lost his way in March; 1 had broken through the ice; and 1 (a woman) was about to be hurled over a bluff by a ruffian.

In addition:

The life-saving crews were called upon during the year to cover considerable miscellaneous property consisting of articles lost overboard from vessels or swept away by the sea, strayed domestic animals, vehicles, and teams involved in bogs and quicksands, etc. Among the objects of material value thus recovered or extricated from difficulty were a bag of United States mail, a gold watch, 23 fish nets, 13 lots of logs and sawed lumber, 5 automobiles 8 buggies and wagons, 15 horses, 3 cows, and 2 hogs.

Visitors to the beach watch the surfmen drill at the Green Run Life-Saving Station. *Courtesy of the Snow Hill Public Library.*

50

Although surfmen staffed these stations primarily during the stormy winter months, skeleton crews were sometimes on hand during the vacation season. The drills conducted by the surfmen provided a pleasant diversion for visitors to the beach. In addition, the surfmen at the Ocean City station, which was within easy walking distance of the Atlantic Hotel, kept a careful watch on the surf and, for more than half a century, became the unofficial lifeguards of the beach.

The Atlantic Hotel proved so popular that in 1880 an addition was built onto the original structure. The *Salisbury Advertiser* reported:

> *The new addition to the Atlantic is now completed and presents a beautiful appearance. It is four stories in height, with a Mansard or French roof, which really makes five stories. The rooms are large and airy, well lighted and ventilated. The halls on the second, third, and fourth floor, are now two hundred and fifty-four feet in length, affording enough room for indoor exercise in inclement weather.*

The Atlantic also added a three-story building to house a bar. According to a report, the Atlantic Hotel "is nearly 300 feet long and stands with one end toward the ocean the other toward the bay, is less than 400 feet from either the bay or the ocean." The additions to the Atlantic Hotel made it the largest and best-appointed hotel on the beach, with accommodations for eight hundred guests. The hotel also had a large kitchen and a dining room that was capable of serving four hundred meals per hour. Across the street, the Massey's Seaside Hotel could accommodate several hundred quests, and the *New York Times* remarked that the "'Lynch' and the Ayers' are also large and well kept houses."

In the year that the Atlantic Hotel expanded, the *New York Times* also commented:

> *The dream of the originators of that seaside city has been fully realized, and what was then a barren waste of sand is now covered by many hotels and private cottages…It offers to the lover of bathing facilities for the gratification of that pleasure second to no other seaside resort on the Atlantic. For the lovers of the surf, the Atlantic Ocean breaks uninterrupted on a sand-bound shore for 40 miles. The undertow, it is claimed is less dangerous that at Atlantic City or at Long Branch, and the certainty of good surf-bathing is absolute, while for the ladies and children who are not strong enough, or do not posses the courage to find pleasure in the breakers,*

By the end of the nineteenth century, Ocean City was rapidly realizing the dream of its founders. *Courtesy of the Delaware Public Archives.*

> *the Synapuxant Bay, which is as close to the hotels as to the ocean, affords perfectly safe bathing in water nowhere over six feet in depth, and in few spots over three feet deep.*

The *New York Times* also pointed out that the moderate prices in Ocean City made the resort attractive to wide range of people. The highest price charged by any hotel in Ocean City was at the Atlantic, where the best rooms could be had for $2.50 a day—and that included meals. The rates for a week's stay in the resort ranged from $8.00 to $12.00.

Unlike many of the older seaside resorts, there was an informality at Ocean City that made the resort seem more like a friendly small town:

> *In the matter of dress, the guests are almost invariably democratic, each lady dresses to suit her own inclination and convenience, and plainness in dress is almost universal, but there is a social element in the society of Ocean City, or at least, there was last season, that is not readily understood*

These ladies dressed to suit their own inclination and convenience. *Courtesy of the Julia A. Purnell Museum.*

by the chance visitors from nearer Northern seaside resorts. The marked and pleasant familiarity between the guests at the hotels is not measured by dress. Nor is there that separation of circles into different sets, as at many other places. The truth is that in Maryland everybody knows everybody.

This informality was fed by the many reunions and conventions that were held in the resort, "where friends could meet friends on common grounds, to entertain and be entertained in strict accordance with the far-famed hospitality of Maryland. Ocean City is a seaside resort within reach of moderate incomes, where health may be recuperated and life may be enjoyed as well as any other point on the Atlantic coast."

Much of the informality of Ocean City stemmed from the female entrepreneurs who opened hotels on the beach. Many years later, Mrs. Edward R. Wilcox recalled in the *Baltimore Sun*:

One of them was my grandmother, Mrs. Rosalie Tilghman Shreve. She founded the Plimhimmon at a time when there were only two other hotels on the beach—the Atlantic and the Seaside—and few cottages. Her husband died of Civil War injuries, and she was faced with the prospect of earning a living for herself and her two sons.

These two vacationers enjoyed ocean bathing at the Ladies' Resort to the Ocean. *Courtesy of the Julia A. Purnell Museum.*

The name of the hotel was taken from the Tilghman family estate at Oxford, Maryland. Shreve's great-grandfather was Tench Tilghman, an aide to General George Washington during the American Revolution. Tilghman was credited with carrying the news of Washington's victory at Yorktown from Virginia to Philadelphia in an epic ride that became a treasured part of Maryland historical folklore. Mrs. Shreve's experience in Ocean City was not unique. In the early twentieth century, a brochure listed twenty-nine hotels and rooming houses—nineteen of these were operated by women, who made Ocean City the "Ladies' Resort to the Ocean."

THE FIRST STEPS ON THE BOARDS

After the Atlantic Hotel was opened and vacationers began to arrive on the coast, it was not long before other buildings were constructed on the beach. In 1894, it was reported in the *Baltimore American* and reprinted in other newspapers that

> [s]*ixty new cottages at Ocean City indicate very clearly that Maryland's great seashore resort is rushing to the front in importance and prosperity. It*

deserves all its success. For a long time Ocean City had to exist largely upon the fact that Bayard Taylor once visited the beach and wrote a few sentences about it in a monthly magazine, but now it is on its own greatness, and its growth will continue.

With so much growth, wooden walkways were built between the new structures to make it easier to walk across the sand. The wooden sidewalks gave Ocean City the appearance of a town out of the Old West, and on the ocean side the resort adopted an idea that had originated in merry old England. Long before Ocean City was established, vacationers in Great Britain traveled to the ports on the English Channel, where they spent the day watching the steady parade of passing ships. At some of the channel ports, wide wooden walkways were erected to enable visitors to get a better view of the steamboats, sailing ships and other passing vessels. By the time that Ocean City had developed into a resort, these boardwalks had become a standard feature at most seaside towns.

Many early Ocean City hotels had been erected on the edges of the dunes, and when the boardwalk was first constructed, there was little

Finely dressed strollers enjoy the early Ocean City boardwalk. *Courtesy of the Julia A. Purnell Museum.*

Two early visitors to the beach sit on the sand in front of a protective wall of pilings. *Courtesy of the Julia A. Purnell Museum.*

distance between the wooden walkway and the surf. In the early days, the boardwalk was put down in sections so that it could be taken up at the end of the summer and stored to prevent damage from winter storms. At that time, the boardwalk was elevated, and it was high enough that a person could easily walk underneath it. In addition, the boardwalk was so close to the breakers that at high tide the ocean washed under the boards. When the tide was out, the area shaded by the boardwalk was a popular meeting place for devotees of the beach. In addition to the boardwalk, rows of pilings were driven into the sand in an effort to keep the sand in place.

For many years, the lack of a wide expanse of sand between the boardwalk and the surf was considered an asset. Most early visitors to Ocean City came to enjoy the sea breezes and take a short ocean "bath." After a hearty breakfast, those hardy souls who wanted to take a dip in the cool Atlantic trudged across the sand to the surf. The *Baltimore Sun* reported in 1894:

> *Ocean City was never more attractive than this summer. The bathing never seemed better, the fish never nibbled at the hook more freely, nor the wind filled the sails more beautifully on Synepuxent bay. This resort, like wine improves with age…there is never a day when it is turbulent enough to repel the most timid bather.*

When vacationers enjoyed a dip in the waves, they did so at their own risk. There were no lifeguards on duty, and many bathers entered the surf in front

The surfmen of the Ocean City Life-Saving Station kept a careful eye on the beach in the event that a swimmer got into trouble. *Courtesy of the Julia A. Purnell Museum.*

of the lifesaving station. As Mrs. N.H. Bittorf, an early visitor to the resort, recalled in the *Baltimore Sun*:

> *Not so many bathers basked and broiled in the sun as people do now. There were bath houses on the boardwalk then, and people would go to them from their rooms to change into their suits—those comic-Valentine things that became heavy as lead when they got wet. From there they would go directly into the ocean—often since there were no lifeguards, into one of the many roped-off "safety" areas. You could wade into the surf, clinging all the while to one of the ropes, and feel perfectly secure.*

After their refreshing dips in the ocean, vacationers quickly crossed the sand to their hotels, where they changed into some of their best clothing for a stroll along the boardwalk. For many years into the twentieth century, the boardwalk was the place to be seen, and everyone dressed accordingly. Ladies wore long dresses and frilly hats. They often carried parasols to avoid getting a tan, which would mark them as a lowly fieldworker. Men wore suits, ties and hats. No one dressed in T-shirts, shorts or the other abbreviated outfits worn by more recent visitors to the boardwalk. According to Bittorf:

As their beaus look on, two ladies tug on what may be one of the safety lines that were strung to protect swimmers. *Courtesy of the Julia A. Purnell Museum.*

Directly behind the pier, on the other side of the boardwalk, was a concession area much like the one there now. There were merry-go-rounds and wheels of fortune and games of skill for which prizes were given. There were also a lot of wheeled chairs or strollers similar to the ones still in Atlantic City. Once a season, various merchants decorated the chairs and started a parade up the boardwalk. That wasn't far, of course.

The early hotels and rooming houses featured wide porches and shady verandas that overlooked unpaved, sandy streets where horses pulled carriages and carts loaded with vacationers and their luggage to their lodgings, which were usually sparsely furnished, lit by oil lamps and equipped with a shiny brass cuspidor. Sanitary facilities consisted of chamber pots and outhouses located behind the main building. Each room had a washstand equipped with pitcher and bowl so that a traveler could freshen up after the dusty trip

Early Ocean City visitors enjoy the sand in front of the resort's rooming houses and hotels. *Courtesy of the Julia A. Purnell Museum.*

to the resort. During Ocean City's early years, windows were left wide open so that cool breezes could flow freely through the room. The windows lacked screens, and to protect the hotel guests from mosquitoes and other insects, rooms were equipped with mosquito netting that hung from fixtures built into the ceilings. In addition to lowering the temperature, the sea breezes also helped ensure that the air was fresh and clean. That was no small matter in the late nineteenth century, when the summer heat, coal-fired industries and animal-pulled vehicles combined to create an urban atmosphere in Baltimore and other large cities that could be staggering. In the early twentieth century, some people hailed the development of the automobile as the answer to the urban air pollution created by the huge number of horses that were used in the large cities.

The sea breeze was a refreshing change from the stale air of the cities, but early Ocean City was far from free of animals. In addition to the horses and oxen that were used for transportation, the lack of an inlet permitted the wild ponies of Assateague to roam freely on the beach. At this time, pony rides on the sand were a popular diversion. Not only were ponies allowed to wander about the resort, but Ocean City did not deem it necessary to ban hogs from the resort until 1915.

When vacationers visited Ocean City during its formative years, they found a small village of charming Victorian buildings perched on the narrow beach. People shared the streets with horses, oxen and other animals, and most folks were just learning how to swim in the surf. Vacationers, however, had no problem negotiating the resort's boardwalk that provided a clean, clear promenade on which they enjoyed the cool sea breeze as they paraded in their fine clothes. A vacationer later recalled in the *Baltimore Sun*:

> *Ocean City was a quieter resort…than it is now. People went primarily to rest: to get good food and good service and to "take the salt air." Dancing became popular. People did a lot of dressing up and parading. Later there were prize-fights, which were favorite events with the men (We girls, dress like Astors, would leave a dance and go to see them just because our husbands wanted to.)*

HARRISON TAKES A GAMBLE

While the buildings of Ocean City were growing like weeds on the dunes of the Maryland coast, Joseph G. Harrison decided that the land around Berlin was more fertile than the beach. In 1885, he surveyed the land around Berlin and decided that nine acres near the railroad station suited his needs, and he bought the land for $3,000 and gambled that he would be able to grow peaches.

After peaches were introduced to America by the Spanish during the sixteenth century, the Native Americans became so enamored of the fruit that they planted peach trees in so many of their villages that some European colonists believed that the fruit had originated in America. As Harrison knew well, during most years peach trees produced abundant and profitable crops, but a severe winter or late frost could ruin an orchard's entire yield. In addition, a blight know as the "yellows" was so virulent that the only known cure was to cut down the orchard and allow the land to remain fallow for several years. Before he bought his land near Berlin, Harrison had seen many peach orchards in southern Delaware succumb to the yellows. Nonetheless, while others were seeking their fortune in Ocean City, he decided to gamble on the land a few miles west of the resort.

Harrison believed that the ocean air would moderate the temperature to allow his peach trees to flourish. In addition, he believed that the railroad would enable him to ship his ripe peaches to the hungry cities of the East Coast. After Harrison planted his orchard and his trees matured, he was rewarded with several years of profitable harvests of peaches. He was also able to acquire additional land in the coastal region. By the beginning of the twentieth century, Harrison began to market nursery stock. Before long he was supplying peach, apple and other trees to orchards throughout the

Workers harvest peaches in one of Harrison's orchards. *Courtesy of the Snow Hill Public Library.*

eastern United States, and he became one of the largest producers of nurse stock in the country. In 1900, he shipped more than 100,000 strawberry plants and fruit trees to other growers. On July 13, 1913, Harrison's nurseries sponsored a huge feast of chicken, ham and watermelon to promote the family orchards. After enjoying the food, the 1,500 guests toured the orchards and listened to lectures on the merits of planting peach trees. Harrison's gamble on the coast had paid off, and soon his family would be looking to Ocean City for additional ventures.

FISHING BY THE POUND

As the resort began to take shape, streets were laid out in a grid pattern and given proper names. North–south streets were named for major cities: Baltimore, Wilmington, Philadelphia, St. Louis and Chicago. Naming two of the resort's major thoroughfares "Baltimore" and "Philadelphia" undoubtedly made vacationers from those two cities feel right at home. At the time that Ocean City was established, St. Louis and Chicago were two forward-looking and expanding towns that gave the resort a sense of progress. Today, Chicago Avenue runs for a few disjointed blocks on the bay side. The boardwalk was thought of as a road that paralleled the ocean, and it was named "Atlantic Avenue."

North and South Division Streets derive their names from the fact that they originally divided the resort from the surrounding beach. Between North and South Division Streets, the east–west roads are named after the counties of the lower Eastern Shore. When the resort expanded beyond the two division streets, the town leaders had apparently exhausted their creativity. The streets between North Division Street and the state line were assigned numbers. The resort's northernmost street is 146th Street, which runs parallel to the border with Delaware, but there are not 146 streets between North Division Street and Delaware. Several numbers were skipped.

When Christopher Ludlam came to town, however, he was more interested in establishing pathways for fish than the roadways that humans took. By the time Christopher Ludlam moved to Ocean City, he had already spent many years living on the Atlantic coast. In the 1880s, Ludlam was the keeper of the Hereford Inlet Life-Saving Station in New Jersey. Ludlam's experience in the service taught him to understand the coast better than most other people did. He knew that large schools of fish migrated along the beach within several hundred yards of the breakers. Ludlam also knew that the resort's rail connections that brought vacationers to the resort could also be used to ship tons of fish to big city markets. Ocean City did not have an inlet at that time, and the only way of reaching the fish would be to launch a boat through the surf.

At the south end of the Ocean City beach, pound fishermen muscled their sturdy boats through the surf. *Courtesy of the Julia A. Purnell Museum.*

Launching a boat through the breakers was a difficult and dangerous task, but Ludlam knew from his years in the U.S. Life-Saving Service that a well-trained crew could muscle a boat through the pounding waves without injury. With his plan firmly in mind, Ludlam had a series of pilings driven into the ocean floor a short distance from the beach. He used these posts to string a system of nets that funneled the fish into a large holding area. Once the fish had been corralled, Ludlam's crews would launch their boats. Unlike the light surfboats used by the service that were designed for easy handling and were not expected to carry heavy loads, the pound fishermen used sturdy boats that would return to shore heavily loaded with the day's catch.

After the seven-man crew muscled the boat across the sand, the fishermen had to slice through the breakers to reach their nets. When the boat arrived at the area where the fish had been collected, the fishermen began the backbreaking work of pulling the nets aboard their small vessel. As they did this, the fish were spilled into the bottom of the open boat. By the time the last section of net was pulled aboard, the men might be standing in a mass of squiggling fish that could be several feet deep.

With the catch safely aboard, the fishermen would head for shore. The return to the beach was the most delicate part of the operation, and any mishap could dump the catch back into the sea. After the boat had safely navigated the surf, it grounded to a halt on the beach. Block and tackle were attached to the boat, and strong Percheron horses were used to pull

Horses helped pull the fishing boats, now heavy with the day's catch, back onto the beach. *Courtesy of the Julia A. Purnell Museum.*

The camp of the pound fishermen, with their poles and boats, stood a short distance south of the Ocean City hotels. *Courtesy of the Julia A. Purnell Museum.*

the fish-laden boat across a series of rollers laid on the sand. After the boat was a safe distance up the beach, the fish were sorted, iced and sent on their way to market. Most of the catch was loaded onto the train for transport to Philadelphia, Baltimore and other cities, but some of the fish were sent to the restaurants in Ocean City.

During the early twentieth century, other entrepreneurs followed Ludlam's example, and there were a dozen pound fishing firms operating on the south edge of the resort. The pound fishing season ran from spring to the fall, and many vacationers hiked across the sand to the small collection of frame buildings that housed the fishermen. The pound fishing camps were so successful that they employed three-quarters of the men working in Ocean City. According to one commentator, "The ocean is compelled to give up its trout and its blue fish and the Synepuxent bay its oysters, clams, crabs, and fish for delectation of the summer visitor's appetite." In addition to enjoying the fishermen's catch on the dinner table, vacationers often spent a few hours at the fishing camp watching the men work with their boats, repairing their nets and doing other chores. Some of the pound fishermen used their boats to take vacationers for a short offshore fishing trip.

ALL THAT WAS ROMANTIC AND EXCITING

Unlike the average Maryland colonist, who saw little worth in living close to the Atlantic Ocean, Samuel Showell saw value in the coastal region, and he acquired eight hundred acres of land on the south shore of the St. Martin's River. Samuel Showell's foresight in investing in the value of northern Worcester County was realized when his descendants continued to assemble additional holdings near the St. Martin's River for farming and timbering. In the late eighteenth century, Lemuel Showell harvested the coastal area's oak, pine and beech trees, and he split the cypress trees that grew in the Great Swamp into shingles. Showell maintained a small flotilla of shallow-draft vessels that carried the timber down the St. Martin's River and across the coastal bay to the Sinepuxent Inlet, where the lumber was offloaded to larger ships for the voyage to distant markets.

When Lemuel Showell died in 1818, his holdings were divided between his seven children, and by the middle of the nineteenth century, one of his grandsons, Lemuel III, was one of the largest landowners on the coast. Lemuel III could have been content to oversee his vast holdings from the back of a black mare—reputed to be one of the fastest horses in the coastal area—but he also inherited his family's keen insight into the value of the region. Lemuel Showell foresaw a time when the railroad would enable the farmers of isolated northern Worcester County to ship their produce to the markets in the major eastern cities in a matter of hours. He also envisioned a time when vacationers would ride the trains to the ocean coast to enjoy a few weeks frolicking in the surf.

Plans to build a railroad in Worcester County were formulated in the 1850s, but construction was delayed by the Civil War. After the war ended, the tracks were quickly laid, and in 1868, the line between Salisbury and Berlin was opened. The first train consisted of a passenger car, a freight car and a small steam locomotive that was appropriately named the *L. Showell*. The passenger car often jumped the track, but fortunately, few people were injured during these mishaps. While some passengers helped to push the car back on to the tracks, others spent their time picking flowers along the right-of-way. These problems did not discourage Showell, who was delighted with the railroad. He was often seen astride his favorite horse galloping alongside the tracks as he raced the train that whisked passengers from Salisbury to Berlin in a mere ninety minutes.

About the time that the railroad between Salisbury and Berlin was constructed, Showell built a small cottage on the beach. At that time,

Lemuel and his guests had to take a horse and carriage from Berlin to the western shore of Sinepuxent Bay, where they boarded a small boat. After being ferried over to the barrier island, Lemuel and his friends had to hike across the sand to his small beach house.

In 1871, Showell began to expand his railroad southward to Snow Hill. This line attracted investors who were assembling a railroad network that ran the length of the Delmarva Peninsula, and he sold his interest in the Snow Hill line for a healthy profit. Showell, who had been an early investor in the Atlantic Hotel, used this money to begin construction on a railroad from Berlin to the ocean. In 1874, a Salisbury newspaper reported:

> *We are happy to be able to announce to our readers that enterprising President and Directors of the Wicomico & Pocomoke Railroad Co. have completed the purchase of the material necessary for the construction of a branch road from Berlin to the sea. The branch will be six miles long, and will afford easy access to one of the most pleasant and popular places of resort on the Peninsula, and enable our citizens and strangers to avoid the tedious stage ride across to the ocean.*

The track from Berlin was completed to the western shore of Sinepuxent Bay in 1874, though vacationers still had to be ferried across the coastal bay. The year after the Atlantic Hotel opened, a railroad trestle that carried a single track was completed across Sinepuxent Bay and terminated in what was known as a "wye," which was a T-shaped arrangement that enabled the train to return across the single track on the Sinepuxent Bridge. When the tracks reached the resort, they turned northward in a gentle curve onto Baltimore Avenue and stopped behind the Atlantic Hotel. A length of track also extended southward toward the pound fishing camps. When the train was ready to leave the resort, it backed southward until the engine was able to turn onto another curved section of track that led back across the bridge and out of town. Using this arrangement, the train could now carry passengers to within a few steps of the accommodations near the beach.

The railroad bridge had a hand-cranked center section that pivoted to allow boats to pass by. When the first horseless carriage appeared, planks were placed on the bridge to allow the early cars to use the bridge in addition to the train. The bridge, however, was so narrow that only one type of vehicle could use the span at a time. Fortunately, both cars and the train traveled at relatively slow speeds when they crossed the bridge; when a train encountered a car going the other way, the horseless carriage had to back up and let the train pass.

When the railroad trestle was completed, the train could pull directly into town, and the railroad was a principal reason for the success of early Ocean City. The railroad carried many vacationers who were staying for the entire summer season. From Washington and Baltimore, the train traveled north around the top of Chesapeake Bay and then southward to the resort. Vacationers boarding trains at Wilmington and Philadelphia, on the other hand, had a much more direct route to Ocean City. As the resort grew and tracks were laid east and west across the Delmarva Peninsula, the train to Ocean City carried visitors who had crossed the bay on steamboats.

In the nineteenth century, the railroad was the fastest way to travel, but a trip from Baltimore to Ocean City was not an easy outing. Vacationers bound for the resort packed a lunch and boarded a boat that headed out of Baltimore harbor at 7:00 a.m. After stops at Annapolis and Bay Ridge to pick up additional passengers, the steamers crossed the Chesapeake Bay. At Claiborne, travelers heading for the resort boarded trains for the dash across the Eastern Shore. Most trains left Claiborne at 9:45 a.m., and they would roll into Ocean City about three hours later. Some trains, such as the Ocean City Flyer, reached speeds of sixty miles per hour and reduced the time of the trip from Claiborne to Ocean City to under two hours.

As the Ocean City Flyer chugged across the Eastern Shore, the speeding train was a treat for residents of small towns along the route. In some small towns, families out for an afternoon stroll gathered at the station to watch the train from Ocean City chug by.

The Ocean City Flyer caught the eye of Kenneth Folks, a young boy in Preston, Caroline County. Many years later, Folks recalled that "the Flyer was a train, and its sole function was the transporting of vacationers to the seaside resort. It was made up of a handsome old-fashioned locomotive which pulled green and gold Pullman cars and maroon-and-gold coaches… that train was the embodiment of all that was romantic and exciting." As the train flashed by, Folks could see the passengers, "wealthy looking and comfortable," as they speeded to Ocean City, "a place which I had never seen and which I envisaged as a sort of paradise."

In the early years, the engines burned pine slabs, which were so bulky that the trains could not carry enough for the trip across the Delmarva Peninsula. The train had to stop at ready-cut lumber piles to "wood up." In 1893, the engines were converted to coal, and this reduced the number of stops. A year later, the railroad lines on the Delmarva Peninsula were consolidated into the Baltimore, Chesapeake and Atlantic Railroad (BC&A). The thick black smoke that billowed from the stacks of the coal-burning engines carried a

During the first three decades of the twentieth century, the train continued to make its way across the trestle into Ocean City. *Courtesy of the Julia A. Purnell Museum.*

shower of embers that blew through the open windows of the passenger cars, earning the BC&A the nickname "Burnt Cinders and Ashes."

When the train reached the railroad trestle that crossed Sinepuxent Bay, conductors circulated through the cars and announced, "All out for Ocean City!" At the train station, there was a cacophony of confusion. In an effort to attract and welcome guests, hotel mangers dispatched brass bands to the station, and the musicians blared out popular tunes. At the same time, vacationers called to porters to help with the baggage and drivers shouted instructions to the horses and oxen that pulled the carriages and carts to the hotels. In addition to the vacationers who stayed in the resort for an extended period of time, the railroad companies ran special excursion trains to the resort. Prices for a round-trip excursion ticket (which was good for five days) from Wilmington were a low as $1.60 and made a trip to the resort attractive to those who could not take an entire summer off.

On Thursdays, the railroad ran day trips to the beach, and the excursion trains chugged into the resort, pulling as many as seventeen cars packed with upward of five thousand people. Edward M. Scott, a resort railroad worker, recalled in the *Baltimore Sun*:

> *Ocean City was a real quiet place then for those who came on the regular trains. Except for "Big Thursday." That was the big excursion day from*

*Wilmington, Claiborne, Cape Charles, and oh, so many places, and they'd
have as many as seventeen coaches on them, bringing crowds of people. It
was a quite a thing for Ocean City on Thursdays.*

Although the tickets for the excursion trains were good for five days, very
few of the riders on these trains stayed overnight in the resort. The excursion
trains came across the Sinepuxent Bridge at about 1:15 p.m. and left at
about 4:00 p.m. the same afternoon, which gave those taking the Thursday
excursion trains under three hours to spend on the beach.

When the extrusion trains pulled in, conditions at the train station would
be chaotic until the crowd had dispersed into the resort. On the other hand,
leaving town was not quite as hectic. The train was scheduled to leave for
Claiborne at 6:20 a.m., but if you had not finished your breakfast, or if you
were a little slow getting to the station, veteran resort visitors knew to sent a
message ahead to the station master to hold the train. Scott recalled:

Vacationers enjoy a sort of paradise in front of Cropper's and Rayne's bathhouses. *Courtesy
of the Delaware Public Archives.*

> *I remember that the train was got ready by Tom Powell…He would come in at 5 in the morning to sweep out the two coaches and the smoker, and when we had it, the parlor car. At 10 past 6 everything was ready—the engineer would blow long blasts on his whistle to notify everybody that the train would go in ten minutes. That was when I would get messages sometimes from Mr. Henry* [the station master] *to hold the train until somebody had finished breakfast.*

When everyone had boarded, however, the train would make its way across the trestle over Sinepuxent Bay to the mainland. With the sun rising over the ocean, the train would pick up speed and leave the "sort of paradise" that was Ocean City behind.

CHAPTER 4

READY FOR VACATION PLEASURES

YOU HAD TO CARRY A LANTERN TO WALK OUT AT NIGHT

At the start of the twentieth century, Ocean City hotels had acquired a well-deserved reputation for their extensive buffets. Breakfast might include fruit, cereal, hominy, fish, soft-shell crab, lamb chops, liver, potatoes, eggs, rolls and corn muffins. The midday meal was the largest meal of the day, and it usually contained generous portions of soup, fish and meat. In the evening, a light supper was served that often included chicken, corn fritters, fish, cold ham, oysters, grits, peas, potatoes, grilled apples, rolls and peaches.

Between meals, vacationers ventured down to the beach, where those who enjoyed a dip in the surf were abandoning the voluminous Victorian bathing attire of the nineteenth century for less cumbersome beachwear. Writing in the *Baltimore Sun*, Frank Henry recalled:

> *By* [the] *next day you were rested and ready for vacation pleasures. The ladies got out their special swimming corsets, which permitted greater freedom of movement while still retaining the illusion of that hour-glass figure. It was best to have two pairs, so you could always have a dry one. If you didn't bring your own swimsuit, the hotel had a variety of them for rent—in the latest style for women—full-skirted, some with circular bands of color in orange, blue, red or brown, and of course, long stockings.*

In the early years of the twentieth century, ladies wore bathing caps, dark stockings and shoes to the beach. *Courtesy of the Julia A. Purnell Museum.*

These ladies have taken a few steps into the surf without holding on to the safety line. *Courtesy of the Julia A. Purnell Museum.*

While still covering all of the torso and extending from the elbows to the knees, the freedom of movement of these newer suits enabled some to do more than bob up and down in the surf. Vacationers were learning to swim at Ocean City.

In many of the hotels, vacationers would gather in the lobby in the morning, listening to someone playing the piano until eleven o'clock, when everyone would change into their bathing attire and head for the beach. After a refreshing ocean bath, vacationers strolled the boardwalk or stopped at the pavilion on the resort's new ocean pier. Completed in 1907, the pavilion featured a long curved roof with distinctive arched windows that provided light for the building's two floors. According to the *Salisbury Advertiser*:

> *One of the greatest improvements Ocean City has ever had is the big ocean pier which is now completed and open to visitors. The new building compares favorably with structures of this class as any of the larger seaside resorts and is a credit to the promoters and builders who had the courage and energy necessary to organize and complete an enterprise of this magnitude.*

The pier pavilion contained a dance hall, a skating rink, bowling alleys, pool tables and assorted refreshment booths. At one time, the ocean end of the pier was used for weeklong trapshooting competitions. Marksmen would shoot at the clay pigeons as they were released over the ocean. At the beach

With the distinctive arched windows of the pavilion, the Ocean City pier formed a backdrop for an early twentieth-century group of vacationers. *Courtesy of the Julia A. Purnell Museum.*

There were only a few wintertime visitors to the resort when this whale was stranded on the beach. *Courtesy of the Julia A. Purnell Museum.*

end of the pier, Rudolph Dolle opened his Candyland shop, where he sold saltwater taffy and other goodies. When motion pictures became popular, they, too, were shown in the pavilion, which also became the backdrop for pictures taken by Ocean City vacationers, who had just begun to bring cameras to the beach.

At the beginning of the twentieth century, photography had come out of the darkroom of the specialist and could be enjoyed by the average person. In its advertisements, the Eastman Kodak Company touted the inexpensive and practical Brownie camera:

> *Ten years ago as practical and satisfactory an instrument as the…Brownie could not have been purchased for less than twenty-five dollars. The Brownie Cameras at one and two dollars each are only made possible by our constant experimental work and by the special machinery which enables us to turn them out by the hundreds of thousands.*

This early visitor to the beach strikes an artful pose for the camera. *Courtesy of the Julia A. Purnell Museum.*

These inexpensive cameras, which resembled a small box with a lens at one end, began showing up on the Ocean City beach, where vacationers took turns taking photographs of one another on the sand.

At about the time that cameras began appearing in the resort, Daniel B. Trimper, who left Baltimore for the resort in 1892, saw a great deal of potential in the resort. Many years later, his son, Daniel Jr., who served as mayor of Ocean City, recalled in the *Baltimore Sun*:

> *None of us could see what father saw in Ocean City at that time. There weren't more than 40 permanent residents here, in contrast to the 1,400 that we have now [1953]. We had none of the bright street lighting then— you had to carry a lantern to walk out at night, and in winter it was spooky when the wind howled around the few houses…In those days it was a tough and long-drawn-out process even to get the doctor over here from Berlin. You'd write him a postcard and maybe for our five days or a week there would come old Dr. Hammond in his horse and buggy. That horse was so old he couldn't eat corn off the cob—I remember I used to shell it off the cob for him.*

This page: These two happy vacationers took turns taking photographs of each other on the beachfront of Rayne's bathhouse. *Courtesy of the Julia A. Purnell Museum.*

After Trimper established Windsor Resort, which included the amusement rides of Luna Park on the boardwalk, he become convinced that his amusement complex needed something exciting, and he decided that Ocean City needed a carousel. At the time, some merry-go-rounds had horses and ponies, made popular by Buffalo Bill's touring Wild West Show. Other carousels featured patriotic themes inspired by American success in the Spanish-American War. The merry-go-round that Trimper erected in Ocean City featured a circus motif that featured lions, zebras and other animals.

Trimper's carousel was crafted by hand by a team of expert woodcarvers. The less-experienced craftsmen would rough out the torso and limbs, and the master carver would add the finishing details, which usually included the expression on the wooden animals' faces. The attention to detail was not unlimited. The left side of each figure, which faced the center of the carousel, tended to be less ornate than the right side of the animal, which faced the outside of the merry-go-round. Of course, the more detailed side of the figure was the side seen by anyone who had not boarded the carousel.

When Trimper came to Ocean City, electricity was a novelty, and he used two generators run by steam engines to create electricity for his park. At that time, amusement parks were festooned with electric lights, and people, most of whom lived in homes lit by oil lamps, came to the park to see the

Trimper's Luna Park with its Ferris wheel and other amusements provided hours of entertainment at the south end of the boardwalk. *Courtesy of the Julia A. Purnell Museum.*

Left: Master craftsmen created this fanciful animal for Trimper's carousel over a century ago. *Photo by Michael Morgan.*

Below: Baltimore Avenue in the early twentieth century before the present city hall was built. *Courtesy of Linda Mitchell.*

lights. Amusement parks liked to illuminate their rides with as many lights as possible. In addition to the lights, the merry-go-rounds were surrounded with mirrors and thousands of pieces of colored glass that turned the spinning carousel into a dazzling display of flashing color and made a ride on Trimper's carousel the highlight of every Ocean City vacation.

While vacationers were focused on the boardwalk, the pier and Trimper's carousel, one of Ocean City's most distinctive buildings was rising at the corner of Baltimore Avenue and Third Street. Authorized by the Maryland General Assembly in 1914, the two-story brick structure was capped by a squat metal dome. Constructed at a cost of $27,000, the building was one of the most expensive erected at the resort. The new dome-topped building was supposed to serve as a college for teachers, but within a year the state had turned the structure over to Worcester County, which used it as an elementary and high school for the children of the resort. The building was expanded during the 1920s and continued to function as a school for another forty years. In 1968, the building was acquired by the City of Ocean City and became the resort's city hall.

A LONELY CAPTAIN ON A HILL

While vacationers were enjoying the sun and surf on the ocean side of resort, Levin Bunting's boats slid effortlessly through the quiet waves of the coastal bay. In the early years of the twentieth century, Captain Levin Bunting maintained a thriving business chartering small boats from his dock on Sinepuxent Bay, near the present Coast Guard Station. Many of the boats Bunting rented to vacationers were built in Bishopville, Chincoteague and other coastal communities. Most of Bunting's boats were small vessels that carried only three or four people. Many of the sailboats were equipped with a centerboard that enabled vacationers to navigate the shallow waters of the coastal bays with ease. The centerboard was lowered to give the vessel stability. When shallow waters were encountered, the centerboard could be raised to keep the small boat from going aground. Occasionally, one of these small sailing craft would slam into a sandbar with such force that the boat could not be refloated. If this occurred, the shallow waters turned into an asset. Passengers just got and waded ashore for help.

The salinity of the coastal bays was low, and during the winter Sinepuxent Bay would be covered with a blanket of smooth, thick ice. During some winters, several of Bunting's boats were fitted with iron runners so that they

Boating on the shallow waters of the coastal bay was a popular diversion at the early resort. *Courtesy of the Julia A. Purnell Museum.*

Shallow-draft sailboats provided a pleasant afternoon on the calm waters of the coastal bay. *Courtesy of the Julia A. Purnell Museum.*

could scoot across the ice-covered bay. Without the inlet, the bay was still fresh water, and it lacked some of the tricky currents that the outlet to the ocean created. But the bay did contain some difficult areas that took an experienced hand to navigate. After several decades sailing the coastal bays, Captain Bunting knew every shoal and shallow.

In addition to his fleet of small craft, Bunting also owned the *Princeton*, and this handsome vessel could carry more than two dozen passengers. Years later, a passenger fondly remembered that "[t]he boats were stately and graceful, unique in design. The old *Princeton* was 45 feet long and could carry about 30 passengers. Ideal for the area, she could sail in the lightest of air and haul up her centerboard to scoot over the shoals. She was a beautiful gaff-rigged catboat with no cabin and a large open cockpit."

Bunting sometimes took vacationers all the way to Chincoteague, Virginia; on other occasions, Bunting took passengers on a guided tour of Assawoman Bay. As the passengers lounged in the open area of the *Princeton*, Bunting provided a running narrative that dealt with ghosts, pirates and local landmarks. When the *Princeton* swung close to the west side of the bay, a small clump of trees could be easily seen on the open grounds of the Ocean City Golf Club. Bunting would point out the trees that stood in the middle of the first fairway, and then he would tell the story of the tragic death of Captain William Carhart.

In January 1799, Captain Carhart set sail from Philadelphia. He had planned to travel to the West Indies and from there to England. As Carhart sailed down the Delaware River and into the Atlantic, a storm was developing in his path off the Maryland coast. Although Carhart wanted to keep his ship far from the beach, the winds from the storm drove him westward toward the Maryland shore. In the days of sailing ships, captains used several ploys to fight contrary winds. They could shorten sail to nearly bare poles to reduce the effects of the wind. They could also deploy a sea anchor, a canvas cone that was supposed to produce enough drag to stall the ship's progress toward shore. If the winds were too strong and continued too long, however, there was little that could be done to prevent the ship from being driven onto the beach.

When Carhart's ship was wrecked on the Maryland coast, the crew and the captain struggled to reach the shore. Although most of the crew members were able to reach the beach safely, Captain Carhart did not. When the surviving crew members found Carhart's lifeless body, they first considered burying their captain on the beach, but after some thought, they concluded that the shifting sands of a barrier island were no place to spend eternity. The crew ferried Carhart's body across Sinepuxent Bay, and after they reached the mainland, they buried Captain Carhart on a low rise safely beyond the bay's marshy shore. Several years after the accident, Captain Carhart's family in England sent both a headstone and footstone to Maryland to mark his grave. For many years, these markers stood alone on the edge of the coastal bay, but eventually, the Ocean City Golf Club was established on the ground that included Carhart's grave.

Captain Carhart's grave is located across the bay from Ocean City in the residential area of Captain's Hill. *Photo by Michael Morgan.*

Bunting would explain how the grave had once been the centerpiece of an annual celebration by a group known as the Camphene Club of Philadelphia, which was Captain Carhart's hometown. Many members of the club belonged to the Philadelphia police force, and they held their annual convention in Ocean City. After the business of the two-day meeting was completed, the club members got down to some serious celebrating. Eschewing the pleasures of the boardwalk and the beach, the members of the Camphene Club climbed into small boats and sailed across the bay to West Ocean City. Once on the mainland, the club band would strike up a tune as a small parade of conventioneers and some local residents made its way to the solitary grave of William Carhart, the English sea captain. At the grave site near the marshy shore of the bay, the club members would break open bottles of beer and drink a toast to Captain Carhart. While the band played a mournful dirge, the Camphene Club would celebrate until the supply of drink was exhausted. None of the Ocean City residents who accompanied the revelries of the Camphene Club ever explained why the club staged this unusual celebration. With his story concluded, Captain Bunting swung the *Princeton* around and headed home.

Driving to the Beach

On July 1, 1904, a horseless carriage owned by Everett E. Jackson finally reached the west bank of Sinepuxent Bay. In the car with Jackson were Allen F. Benjamin of Salisbury and J. Edgar Igams, the owner of an Ocean City hotel. As the three men looked across the bay to their destination, they concluded that the only way to reach Ocean City was to carefully guide their vehicle onto the railroad trestle and hope that they reached the other side before a train arrived. A few minutes later, the trio arrived on the other side of the trestle, and they rode the first car on to the streets of Ocean City.

The pioneering auto travelers had made the thirty-mile journey from Salisbury in only four hours and eighteen minutes. On several occasions, the trio was forced to stop for minor repairs, and at one point between Willards and Whaleysville, they had to stop to allow their overheated engine to cool down. Jackson and his two friends also ran off the road twice.

At that time, the roads of Worcester County were designed for animal-pulled vehicles and bicycles. In the last decade of the ninetieth century, Americans became obsessed with bicycles. New "safety" bikes with two wheels of equal size made bicycling easy for everyone. At the turn of the century, biking become so popular that many Maryland roads were covered with a layer of crushed stone to give bicyclists a better surface on which to ride. At the same time, many of the farmers in Worcester County and other rural areas had lobbied for better roads that would enable them to more easily ship their produce to market.

When Jackson, Igams and Benjamin set out on their historic journey from Salisbury to Ocean City, their horseless carriage reached a top speed of thirty miles per hour, and as it bounced along the stone-covered road, the car generated a billowing cloud of dust. Three years after Jackson drove into Ocean City, state road officials offered two ideas to deal with the dust problem. All cars, state bureaucrats suggested, should be equipped with a governor to prevent them from going fast enough to generate a dust cloud. If this plan was rejected, state road officials suggested that speed bumps be installed at appropriate intervals across all Maryland highways to keep the speed of cars in check.

Fortunately for future drivers to Ocean City, highway officials discovered that a bituminous surface applied over crushed-stone roads effectively kept the dust under control. A decade after the first car reached Ocean City, road crews were busy applying a bituminous surface to some of the roads that led to the resort. The hard-surfaced roads made travel by car much easier,

These two Worcester County gentlemen would have been disappointed if speed bumps had been installed on the road to Ocean City. *Courtesy of the Julia A. Purnell Museum.*

but the new roads also required constant maintenance. To keep the roads in good repair, the state developed a system of "district engineers" to monitor the condition of the road surface. These men were issued motorcycles, and they spent much of the time riding around looking for holes to fill. In addition to the district engineers, each mile in the state road system was assigned to a patrolman. The patrolmen lived on or near the roads in their care. The patrolmen wore caps emblazoned with the words "State Patrolman," and they carried red flags to warn motorists of their presence as they pushed a wheelbarrow filled with a supply of bituminous material and stones to patch the roads. Patrolmen earned between $2.00 and $2.50 a day, and they were part of the state road maintenance system until 1930.

Snow removal was another new problem created by the hard-surfaced roads. Although snow made travel by animal-pulled wagons on unpaved roads more difficult, it was nearly impossible for cars to negotiate the snow-covered bituminous roads. When it was first suggested that the state spend money to remove the snow, many people objected on the grounds that it was a waste of taxpayers' money. After all, the snow would eventually melt. By 1922, the state had conducted tests on the effect of snow on the hard-surface highway. It was discovered that the cost of repairing the damage done by snow left to melt on the road was greater than the cost of removing the snow. The data was so convincing that snow removal became an accepted part of road maintenance.

As roads improved, more and more people preferred to drive to Ocean City. When Jackson and his cohorts drove the first car into Ocean City in 1904, the vast majority of visitors to the resort arrived by train. It would be two decades later when cars would carry most visitors to the resort, and the train would soon become a relic of the past.

HIDDEN DANGERS

In April 1917, Ocean City was preparing for the start of another summer season when the resort's residents discovered that the Maryland beach had attracted an unwanted visitor: war. The resort had been established and developed with little thought that an enemy warship could appear off the coast and begin lobbing shells into town. That changed in April 1917, when the United States declared war on Germany.

When America entered World War I, coastal residents understood the dangers of modern warfare. German submarines had torpedoed hundreds of ships (including the passenger liner *Lusitania*) in European waters. In addition, Germany had demonstrated that its U-boats could reach the Maryland coast. In 1915, the submarine *Deutschland* eluded the British navy, and it crossed the Atlantic. The United States was still at peace with Germany when the *Deutschland* arrived at the mouth of Chesapeake Bay. The submarine had

As did most folks before World War I, these two couples dressed well for a visit to the beach. *Courtesy of the Julia A. Purnell Museum.*

been outfitted as a cargo vessel, and it carried $6 million worth of dyes on its voyage to America. After the *Deutschland* reached the mouth of the bay, it sailed north to Baltimore, where an enthusiastic crowd greeted it.

When the United States declared war against Germany in 1917, the news of the voyage of the *Deutschland* was still fresh in the minds of many Worcester County residents. Many correctly believed that submarines could be lurking in Maryland's coastal waters. In June 1918, the French merchant ship *Radioleine* and the schooner *Edward Baird* were cruising off the Maryland coast when they were attacked by a German submarine. Although submarines at that time were equipped with torpedoes, U-boat captains preferred to save them for use against warships. When a submarine came upon unarmed merchant ships, submarine commanders usually brought their vessel to the surface and attacked with their deck guns. In this case, the submarine made easy work of the wooden schooner, which soon started to slip beneath the waves. After the U-boat crew turned its attention to the French ship, an American destroyer appeared on the scene. According to an official statement issued later that day that appeared in the *New York Times*:

> The Navy Department has received a dispatch from a United States destroyer stating that at 9:30 this morning she interrupted an attack by an enemy submarine on the French steamer Radioliene, about sixty-five miles off the coast. The destroyer also took on board two men from the Edward Baird, which was bombed and sinking.

The *Radioliene* was able to reach port safely as the navy attempted to find the submarine that attacked it. According to the *New York Times*:

> The vessels closing in on the submarine that attacked the Radioliene are expected to acquit themselves gloriously, if, as flashed unofficially tonight the submarine is being chased along the Maryland shore. If the submarine can be forced toward the shore, many shallow places will be found where an undersea boat of large size would not be able to submerge.

Despite the navy's efforts, however, the U-boat was able to slip away from the Maryland coast.

Shortly after the attack on the *Radioliene*, the German submarine *U-117* arrived in Maryland waters. The deck gun of the enemy submarine was capable of blasting holes in the Ocean City boardwalk, and a single torpedo from a German U-boat could sink most ships cruising along the Maryland coast. The captain of the *U-117* had been given a different mission. As the *U-117* sailed along the coast, the submarine deposited several dozen mines.

The deadly German mines rode quietly in Maryland waters until they were struck by an unsuspecting vessel. The battleship *Minnesota* hit one of these devices, and it was damaged by the resulting blast. The warship's heavy metal plating enabled it to make its way safely to Philadelphia, but the merchant ship *Saetia*, commanded by Captain W.S. Lynch, was not so lucky. On November 9, 1918, the merchant ship was sailing through heavy seas when it was rocked by an explosion. The blast from the mine knocked several crewmen into the cold ocean. The captain of the *Saetia* ordered "all hands on deck," but the damage to the ship was so great that the vessel began to slip beneath the waves.

As the crew struggled to launch the lifeboats, water cascading into the *Saetia* swamped the ship's boilers, which exploded. At Ocean City, members of the Coast Guard launched a small rescue vessel through the heavy surf. In addition, several ships in the vicinity raced to the rescue. The *New York Times* reported:

> *The sinking was preceded by an explosion a few minutes after 8 o'clock. A few minutes later two more explosions followed, both violent. Although the ship was light, she went down within twenty minutes…Coast Guard cutters and a number of destroyers rushed to the aid of the steamship, which submerged before any could come alongside. A number of the crew were picked up in the water. The sea was very rough.*

After the *Saetia*'s crewmen were plucked from the ocean water, several of the ship's lifeboats were escorted to the Ocean City beach. The heavy surf made it difficult to land the rescued sailors, but eventually several dozen men reached the beach. The *New York Times* reported:

> *The survivors landed here were scantily clad. They were greatly fatigued, having been several hours in the water. Their weakened condition was aggravated by the six-hour ride in the small boats, which were like corks on the heavy seas. The Seaside Hotel has been turned over to the local chapter of the Red Cross. There the survivors will be fed, clothed, and sheltered by the town, with the co-operation of the Red Cross. Among those at the hotel is Captain Lynch, who stood by his ship to the last.*

The sinking of the *Saetia* was a chilling reminder to the people of Ocean City that the war had come to its shores. Fortunately for the resort, World War I came to an end two days after the *Saetia* was sunk.

CHAPTER 5

OCEAN CITY WEATHERS THE STORMS

WAR ON TURF

The rapid industrialization of the United States following the Civil War helped create an affluent middle class that could enjoy a week at the ocean and a day at the races. By the early years of the twentieth century, Ocean City had developed into a flourishing seaside resort, and horse racing had emerged as one of America's most popular spectator sports. After the outbreak of World War I, New York financier August Belmont II became caught up in the patriotic fervor of the war. The sixty-five-year-old horse fancier enlisted in the army, and his wife picked out one of Belmont's yearlings; in a romantic gesture, she named it "My Man o' War."

At the same time that Belmont was marching off to war (his principal duty entailed securing mules for the army), Samuel Riddle arrived on the Maryland coast, where he believed that "[t]he salt air and bluegrass of Worcester County" was ideal for raising horses. Riddle established a horse farm on the mainland just west of Ocean City on Herring Creek. Riddle planned to raise show and hunting horses, and he immediately began to turn his Worcester County farm into a sumptuous estate. The farmhouse was converted into a grand twenty-five-room manor house where Riddle could entertain the many visitors who would come to see his horses. Soon after he made his first purchase, Riddle decided that the area was better suited to raising racehorses. Eventually, Riddle's farm contained more than one thousand acres just off the road that ran from Berlin to Ocean City. He built a main stable longer than a football field, several smaller stables, workers'

A horseshoe-shaped memorial to Man o' War sits amid the golf courses and new homes west of Ocean City. *Photo by Michael Morgan.*

quarters, houses for guests, a carriage house, a $3,000 doghouse for his sixty-five foxhounds and a private dock on Turville Creek. At the entrance to his estate, Riddle built a private, winding road that he lined with $1,000 worth of shrubbery. To stock his new farm, Riddle bought several colts from August Belmont. Among these was the horse that Belmont's wife had named when her husband joined the army. By the time the big red horse arrived at Riddle Farm, his name had been slightly shortened to "Man o' War."

In the spring, the horses would arrive from Kentucky, and the trainers would put the thoroughbreds through a rigorous training schedule. As the horses began to arrive, so did visitors to the farm. Some were Riddle's guests; other visitors came to enjoy the wide green lawns and the sight of the horses exercising on the estate's mile track. Once the horses were properly conditioned, half were sent to race at tracks in the North and the other half to southern tracks.

Man o' War won every race that he entered, and some of the victories were won by incredibly wide margins. Some believed that the horse was unbeatable, but in August 1919, Riddle entered Man o' War in the Sanford Stakes at Saratoga Springs. The *New York Times* reported the shocking result: "The Glenn Riddle Farm's great two-year-old, Man o' War was next to the outside heels of a rival in his first six races, met with his first defeat here today in the running of the Sanford Memorial." The horse that scored this surprising victory over Glenn Riddle Farm's champion was appropriately named "Upset."

Two weeks later, Man o' War faced Upset again, and according to the *New York Times*:

> *Glen Riddle Farm's Man o' War will go down in the history of this year's racing as the king of the two-year-old division. This great son of Fair Play proved today that he is an exceptional colt, and in a class by himself, when he galloped away with the rich Grand Union Hotel Stakes of $10,000 at six Furlongs. He not only won handily, but he avenged the single defeat of his career by taking the measure of his recent conqueror, Upset, beating him to the wire by two lengths.*

When Man o' War returned to Maryland for a vacation at his Worcester County home, crowds of motorists drove by Riddle Farm on their way to Ocean City, and after the summer crowds were gone, Man o' War continued to romp through the fields at Riddle Farm. When the spring of 1920 arrived, Riddle did not enter his once-beaten champion in the Kentucky Derby, but Man o' War handily won the Preakness.

The *New York Times* boldly stated: "At the conclusion of the Preakness some experienced horsemen expressed the opinion that Man o' War is undoubtedly the greatest colt that this country has produced in a score of years, if indeed he is not the greatest racer the country has ever seen." At the end of the racing season, Riddle retired Man o' War—voted the "Horse of the Century."

For several decades after Man o' War was put out to stud, Riddle Farm remained the center of social events. The farm was often crowded with sportsmen who enjoyed hunting for geese and ducks in the coastal bays. In addition, Riddle staged fox hunts on Assateague Island. After World War II, Ocean City continued to experience rapid growth, but horse racing had begun to lose its luster. Riddle died in the 1950s, and his once great horse farm went into a long decline. In 1978, the last of the horses were shipped away, and the home of Man o' War, the coast's most famous resident, was closed.

RUMRUNNERS STORM THE COAST

When World War I came to an end in 1918, the Coast Guard, which had succeeded the U.S. Life-Saving Service in 1915, ended its patrols along the beach, and ships sailed along the coast without fear of attack. After a mild adjustment to peacetime conditions, the economy boomed, and during the 1920s, vacationers flocked to the resort in record numbers. Ocean City began to roar along with the rest of the country.

When American soldiers returned from Europe after World War I, they reported that French women were not wearing stockings while swimming. In Ocean City, women also began wearing swimsuits that exposed much of the legs and all of the arms. In addition, men began to enter the surf topless! Some in Ocean City found the new styles controversial, but the modern swimsuits were soon a common sight on the resort's beach.

The bustling postwar economy, improved roads and a new highway bridge over Sinepuxent Bay made it easier for many families to drive to Ocean City.

After a highway bridge was completed over Sinepuxent Bay, motorists had an easier time driving to the resort. *Courtesy of the Delaware Public Archives.*

During the 1920s, drivers in the resort had only a few streets to explore. At the beginning of the decade, the town ended north of Third Street, but the influx of visitors drove the resort steadily northward, and the buildings used by the pound fishermen discouraged expansion south of town. The war, however, had brought hard times to the fishing camp. Before World War I, there were eight commercial fishing operations located just south of Ocean City. By the end of the war, this number had dropped to two, and by the end of the 1920s, commercial fishing was declining along the Maryland coast.

During the carefree decade following World War I, the Eighteenth Amendment to the Constitution went into effect and outlawed the manufacture and sale of alcoholic beverages. The United States was officially "dry," but many people openly flaunted the law. As one coastal resident recalled, "I remember them having these stills in the woods where they wasn't supposed to make liquor, and every once in a while, the federal men would catch them."

On another occasion, a cache of bottles was confiscated by government agents who believed that they contained bootleg whiskey. When the bottles were opened, the law enforcement officials were embarrassed by the familiar smell of another liquid. The coastal bootleggers had gotten wind of the raid, and the offending moonshine had been replaced with coffee.

During the Prohibition era, shipments of booze were loaded aboard small vessels in Canadian ports. Whiskey, gin and other alcoholic spirits were packed in rectangular metal containers that could be easily stacked on a small boat. Often the metal tins were covered with a cloth sack so that they could

The grassy dunes of Ocean City provided a convenient landing place for bootleggers. *Courtesy of the Delware Public Archives.*

be handled quietly. Once loaded, the boat would leave Canadian waters and sail down the East Coast, where the rumrunner would anchor a safe distance from the shore. The tins of alcohol would be loaded onto a small boat that was run through the surf onto the beach, where it was reloaded onto trucks and transported to speakeasies in Washington, Baltimore and elsewhere.

In December 1929, the approach of New Year's Eve presented an irresistible opportunity for the whiskey smugglers. One late December morning, an off-duty police officer noticed a suspicious boat hovering near the shore a short distance south of the resort. The policeman immediately notified the men of the Ocean City Coast Guard Station at Caroline Street and the boardwalk. Within minutes, the Coast Guardsmen swooped down on the smugglers and arrested the men on the beach. As usual, the mother ship was able to slip away in the night. Although this landing—which featured whiskey, gin and champagne supposedly made in France—was stopped, boatswain's mate Garwood J. Thomas took one of the skiffs that had been used to land the liquor, dragged it across the sand and launched it into the coastal bay. He crossed the bay to Coffin's Point, not far from Ocean City, where he found a building piled high with cases of booze. In addition, there was a truck half-filled with more bootleg liquor. With the help of the state police and additional men from the Coast Guard, 1,850 cases of booze were confiscated, and two men were arrested. The booze from the beach and mainland (which had an estimated value of $250,000) was hauled back to the Caroline Street Coast Guard Station, but there was not enough room inside the station to store the whiskey. The tins of bootleg liquor had to be stacked around the station, making the building look as if it had been sandbagged against a monster high tide.

The bootleggers, most of whom came from the Ocean City area, were hauled off to Easton, where the jail became so crowded that cots were set up in the lobby. The ringleaders were sentenced to two years in prison, and others got lesser sentences. Many of their families appealed the incarcerations, contending that they would become destitute, but the judge refused to waver. The residents of the resort raised money for the relief of the families, and this effort was so successful that one newspaper reported, "It is being used to keep the wolf from the door of the wives and children while the fathers and husbands are in jail."

The ambivalent public support for prohibition was best expressed by the men of the Coast Guard, who were charged with a dual mission of pulling people from the surf and stopping the flow of bootleg liquor. One commented, "If you weren't rescuing 'em, you were arresting 'em."

An Awful Sound

"Fire! Fire!"

The ringing of the town's fire bell sent shivers down the spines of those who heard it. As a resident of Worcester County once recalled, the fire bell was "an awful sound" that signaled the discovery of a blaze out of control. The coastal sea breezes could turn a minor fire into a major conflagration, as the residents of Berlin, Ocean City's neighbor to the west, learned in 1895. Berlin's excellent rail connections made it a thriving business center of several thousand residents. On Sunday evening, August 10, 1895, a fire began in a stable and quickly spread to nearby buildings. The wind shifted and ignited Berlin's old downtown Atlantic Hotel, which burned to the ground.

After the fire, the town passed an ordinance that mandated that buildings constructed to replace burned businesses had to be made of brick. Shortly after the fire, a new Berlin Atlantic Hotel was constructed, and when completed, the three-story brick structure had an impressive ninety-foot exterior punctuated by high windows with decorative iron lintels. A covered porch ran the length of the front of the building that faced on a small open area of Main Street. When it was opened, a Snow Hill newspaper declared,

After the fire had destroyed its predecessor, Berlin's new Atlantic Hotel was built of brick. *Photo by Michael Morgan.*

"It be truly said that Berlin now has one of the largest, handsomest, and best equipped hotels on the Eastern Shore."

The fire in Berlin had taught that town a hard lesson that the people of Ocean City were slow to notice, and this neglect put the resort's oceanfront Atlantic Hotel in jeopardy. When Ocean City was established in the nineteenth century, citizens responded to the cry of "Fire!" by forming a bucket brigade to fight the blaze. As Ocean City grew, many residents recognized the need for better protection against fires. In 1905, a fire company was organized, and it held meetings in the old Methodist tabernacle on Dorchester Street. The town of Ocean City had purchased the church building to serve as a jail and to house city offices. Shortly after the new fire company began to meet there, it suffered its most embarrassing setback when the building was destroyed by fire. In spite of these early difficulties, the Ocean City firefighters soon established a first-class fire company.

In just a few decades, the town had changed from being a sleepy collection of cottages and rooming houses to a modern resort. In addition, the town had become electrified. A generating plant at Somerset Street and Baltimore Avenue provided power for electric lights, neon signs and all of the resort's electrical appliances.

On a cold winter morning in 1925, a heavy wind was blowing from the ocean, and sparks were spitting out of the power plant. The sparks soon ignited a fire, and the steady sea breeze sent glowing embers to other buildings. Anne Bunting, who operated a small rooming house, saw the fire when it first started: "I saw it when it wasn't as big as a bushel basket. I could see it because I was standing on my back porch and there weren't any houses behind me." When the fire reached the Seaside Hotel, the wind fanned the flames into a glowing inferno.

The Ocean City fire company responded quickly to the first alarm, but when the firefighters arrived on the scene, they discovered that many of the hydrants were frozen. As the firefighters struggled to free the hydrants, a call for help was sent out to nearby towns. Fire companies from Berlin, Snow Hill, Pocomoke and Salisbury rushed toward Ocean City as the resort's firefighters battled the spreading blaze, heavy winds and frozen hydrants.

Soon, flames could be seen leaping out of the Atlantic Hotel. An eyewitness recalled, "The fire just kept blazing away. It burned the electric light plant, then it skipped across the street and burned the laundry at the Atlantic Hotel and it burned the whole Atlantic Hotel and some buildings on Wicomico Street."

Anne Bunting saw the flames spreading toward Dr. Townsend's Washington Pharmacy on the boardwalk at Somerset Street. Townsend was a native of

In this image of an uncrowded boardwalk, Townsend's Washington Pharmacy can be seen to the left behind the people with umbrellas. *Courtesy of the Julia A. Purnell Museum.*

Snow Hill who married Anna Ryane, whose family owned the Ryane Hotel and several other resort businesses. Bunting and a dozen other women snatched bedsheets from their homes and descended on the pharmacy, which was the resort's principal source of medicines. After each sheet was filled with a pile of bottles, boxes and drugs, they were dragged to safety.

Years later, Anne recalled that "[w]e were going by the wind. It stayed to the southwest and carried the fire more to the boardwalk. You had to learn those things if you live on an island."

Although the fire was extinguished before it reached the pharmacy, other Ocean City landmarks were not so lucky. The conflagration had destroyed the Atlantic Hotel, the Seaside Hotel, the Winter Gardens, Dolle's Candyland, the pier pavilion, the Casino Theatre and a substantial portion of the boardwalk. It would not take long for Ocean City to recover from the 1925 fire, though. The Atlantic Hotel was rebuilt, and the pier pavilion was replaced with a two-story building that featured high windows on the second floor but lacked the distinctive arches that had been a feature

During the 1920s, construction boomed in Ocean City. *Courtesy of the Delaware Public Archives.*

of the first pavilion. The resort quickly jumped back into step with the Roaring Twenties, but resort residents who saw the blaze burning out of control remembered that the pealing of a fire alarm could truly be "an awful sound."

A Place to Stay

While the damaged buildings from the 1925 fire were being repaired and rebuilt, summer crowds continued to flock into the resort, and some of Ocean City's hotels hired African Americans to work as maids and porters who had worked in Florida during the winter. Ocean City was a segregated town, and African Americans were not allowed on the boardwalk except on "Colored Excursion Days" after the summer season closed on Labor Day. To house their workers, the hotels often provided bare-bones accommodations that sometimes lacked running water for these workers. Years later, an African American who worked in one of the hotels recalled, "Yet you were expected to come to the dining room strictly clean. One washbowl down there with the whole crew down there. They didn't have a shower until we complained so much about it. Just one faucet and that was cold."

Despite being in the resort during the vacation season, the black workers saw little of the surf and sand. Elsie Ewell recalled in *Worcester Memories*, "We stayed the whole summer and we worked every day, and then we were all even on call. We had to be on call at night. And if you went up on the boardwalk, you would get pushed off." The Pier Ballroom, however, hosted some of the great musicians of the Roaring Twenties, including prominent black musicians Cab Calloway, Duke Ellington and Count Basie. These entertainers would not have been able to stay in Ocean City had it not been for Charles T. Henry, a mail carrier and the area's first African American school bus contractor.

In 1926, Henry bought a small hotel on the corner of South Division Street and Baltimore Avenue from a white businessman, and the next year, Henry's Colored Hotel opened. The full-service hotel with its laundry and restaurant provided accommodations and services for African American visitors to Ocean City that could not be found anywhere else in the resort. Across the street from the hotel, which Henry operated with his wife, Louisa, was the nightclub Grand Terrace—like many establishments in Ocean City, it also operated a gambling hall. The Grand Terrace, however, catered to both black and white patrons.

A Storm Changes the Face of Ocean City

In 1933, Ocean City was over half a century old and growing larger every year. Even the massive unemployment of the Great Depression did not slow the steady parade of vacationers to Maryland's ocean coast. If Ocean City had a drawback, it was the lack of a waterway between the ocean and the coastal bays. One by one, the inlets that once led across Assateague Island to Chincoteague Bay had silted shut, and by the 1930s, the inlets were gone, and Assateague Island was a continuous ribbon of sand that extended the entire length of the Maryland coast.

There were calls for the creation of a new inlet, but an attempt to dig an inlet before World War I ended in failure, when the shallow waterway quickly silted closed. Following the war, the State of Maryland appropriated $500,000 to cover two-thirds of the cost of digging a new inlet, and the leaders of Ocean City lobbied the federal government for the rest of the funds to construct a new waterway. In 1933, Congress postponed consideration of a bill to provide the resort with the inlet funds, and it seemed that the project was doomed.

Bands paraded along the boardwalk during the 1930s. *Courtesy of the Julia A. Purnell Museum.*

While the people of Ocean City hoped for support with its inlet project, visitors to Public Landing seemed content. Situated on the western shore of Chincoteague Bay, Public Landing was located due east of Snow Hill, and the bayside resort had been attracting vacationers long before the first hotel was built in Ocean City. In the nineteenth century, visitors to Public Landing enjoyed picnicking, crabbing and boating on the calm waters of the coastal bay. For many years, well-heeled vacationers dressed in their finest apparel for a walk along Public Landing's boardwalk and pier. In addition, the resort boasted a dance hall, merry-go-round, a bowling alley, a theater and other amusements. At that time, swimming was just coming into vogue, and quiet Chincoteague Bay was perfect for people who were taking their first recreational dip in the water.

By the beginning of the twentieth century, Ocean City was attracting more vacationers than Public Landing, but many people remained loyal to the bayside resort. Ocean City was crowded in August 1933 when a weekend rain convinced many vacationers to head home. After dropping an estimated ten inches of rain, the storm continued to intensify. Vacationers who had hesitated leaving the resort discovered that the rising bay water had inundated the highway bridge that sat a short distance north of the old railroad trestle. With the road out of town blocked, the last visitors to flee Ocean City were ferried across the bay in small boats.

With the highway bridge and the railroad trestle submerged, the resort was effectively cut off from the mainland. High winds drove heavy waves surging across the sand and crashing into the boardwalk. South of town, the storm uprooted the poles that held the pound fishing nets, and the waves raced across the beach to destroy the wooden buildings of the fishermen.

In Ocean City, the surf rolled over the dunes, and the water cascaded into the city's streets. The boardwalk began to splinter, and buildings buckled under the pounding of the waves. While the ocean waves ate into the beach from the east, the bay water steadily eroded the island from the west. Near daybreak, a large wave lifted a section of the boardwalk off its pilings and washed large timbers into the streets. As the erosion of the beach at the deserted south end of town continued to push bayward, the accumulated water in the coastal bay began to pinch the barrier island. Finally, the sand gave way, and a short distance from South Division Street, the pent-up bay water gushed through a new inlet toward the ocean.

When the storm finally subsided, a crew from the Coast Guard Station used a surfboat to navigate through the resort's flooded streets, and they rescued several people trapped in flooded buildings. Mountains of debris from the boardwalk, houses and other structures had been deposited throughout the town. After the damaged was surveyed, Mayor W.W. McCabe put one hundred men to work repairing the dismembered boardwalk, clearing the sand and debris from the resort's streets and restoring power to the damaged street lights. McCabe optimistically announced that "Ocean City will be ready for business as usual by late this afternoon or tomorrow."

Ocean City would be open for vacationers before the end of the 1933 season, but it would not be "business as usual." The highway bridge had been damaged, but the State Roads Commission repaired the structure, and vehicles were able to reach the resort without difficulty. On the other hand, the train trestle had been carried away by the storm, but the trestle was not rebuilt. Edward Scott, a ticket agent for the railroad, recalled:

> *When you look at things in a long way the era of the railroad was pretty short. It started in 1879 and wound up in 1933—a period of 54 years. Of course, the railroad wanted to discontinue service long before the*

During the 1930s, visitors to the boardwalk braved the sea breezes. *Courtesy of the Julia A. Purnell Museum.*

hurricane of '33 washed away the bridge. Why, I sold only two tickets to passengers in May of 1933, and in June of that year, a vacation month, I sold just five tickets.

With the bridge gone, rail service to the resort was permanently ended. In addition, the pound fishing camp had also been destroyed and would not be rebuilt.

The inlet created by the storm was stabilized, and within a short time, sport and commercial fishermen were setting sail from Ocean City. Five years after the storm, Every McBee, a resident of the resort, recalled in the *Baltimore Sun*:

A pair of adventurous brothers—the Townsends—steered their little craft out to sea. Twenty-five miles they went, casting here and there before a sail-like fin cleared the ocean surface and felt the strike of a mighty fish. There rang a cry that caused the great of all sporting fraternities to prick up its ears—"Marlin at OC!" And ever since anglers have arrived in increasing

The new inlet enabled Ocean City to become a center for deep-sea fishing. *Courtesy of the Delaware Public Archives.*

> *numbers to battle the great sailfish, with sword-like snouts, and the game bluefish that swam off the coast.*

The most devastating storm to hit the resort had created an opportunity for deep-sea fishing that added yet another dimension to the growing resort, which had avoided the flash and dash of other resorts. As McBee recalled in 1938:

> *There will be no bathing beauty pageants, no baby parades, no million dollar piers, no widely ballyhooed events, no mammoth conventions and no tinseled entertainment on the shores of Worcester County this summer; there never have been. While other resorts are priming their pumps with publicity dollars, OC will be quietly unlocking its doors and pointing with modest pride at its new apartment buildings and cottages and a few harbor improvements. And that (plus the sand and the ocean) is what the summer visitors wish.*

The 1933 storm turned many of the buildings at Public Landing into matchsticks. *Courtesy of the Snow Hill Public Archives.*

South of Ocean City, at Public Landing, the story was quite different, where many of the bayside resort's buildings had been reduced to matchsticks. Most of the amusements were not rebuilt, and today Public Landing has a parking area, a boat ramp and a wooden pier that Worcester County residents use to enjoy the area's natural assets.

MORE CARS THAN YOU CAN COUNT

After the inlet was created, a growing number of deep-sea fishermen began using Ocean City as their home port. As the Fourth of July week in 1937 approached, a solid line of cars stretched from the Route 50 Bridge toward Berlin. The vehicles seemed to move along for a short time, and then the cars would inexplicably come to a dead stop. Many drivers became so frustrated over their inability to reach the resort that they pulled off the road and spent a pleasant weekend exploring the back roads of Worcester County.

The vacationers who persevered on Route 50 spent two hours inching along the road toward their destination. When the motorists finally reached the western side of Sinepuxent Bay, they discovered the culprit who was causing the resort's first major traffic jam. At the Route 50 Bridge, the line of cars making their way into the resort intersected with a parade of fishing boats heading for the inlet. Much to the fury of those in their cars, Paul Parker, the bridge tender, was forced to stop the car traffic and open the bridge for the fishermen. To leave the bridge down would cause a backup of fishing vessels waiting to get to the sea. Despite the growing frustrations of both drivers and seamen, Parker remained faithfully at his post and alternately allowed fishermen and sun worshipers to reach their destinations. When the bridge was lowered and the cars began to move again, Parker passed the time by counting each vehicle as it passed by. By the end of the weekend, he had counted twelve thousand cars that had taken several hours to drive from Berlin to Ocean City.

Driving to Ocean City had always been a chore. Motorists from the Baltimore-Washington area had to endure a slow ferry ride across the bay, poor roads and congested towns to reach the resort. According to one commentator, "The hard part is the trip across the shore, and it is hard on account of the lack of a first-class road, comparable to the Ritchie Highway."

In 1939, a modern highway along the coast opened, providing a direct link between Ocean City and the Delaware resorts. The coastal road enabled Ocean City to begin a steady expansion northward across nearly ten miles of natural dunes to the Delaware line. When the road was opened, there were only a few scattered buildings in this area that had been home to beachcombers and scavengers.

A few years before Ocean City was established, David James Long of Selbyville visited Fenwick Island and the northern Maryland coast. When Long arrived on the beach, there were just three houses there. According to Long, "We found three dwellings, all houses occupied. In the first house we found a widow, Zippy Lewis, her skin browned by the sun. We had our dinner with her. It is reported that she had a lot of beach money buried on the island somewhere."

In the middle of the nineteenth century, Zippy married Jonathan B. Lewis of Williamsville, Delaware, and the young couple built a small cottage on Fenwick Island, which at that time included part of the Maryland coast. Zippy and Jonathan spent much of their time salvaging timber from wrecked vessels and using the reclaimed lumber to build their house. Then, one day, Jonathan decided to go to sea.

The beach and marshes where Zippy Lewis once maintained her shack, as seen from the top of the Fenwick Island Lighthouse. *Courtesy of the Delaware Public Archives.*

After her husband left, Zippy supposedly went down to the beach every day to watch in vain for his return. As the years passed, Zippy became a familiar figure to the growing number of people who visited the beach after the Civil War. Wearing a long dress and sunbonnet, Zippy scavenged the beach for anything of value. With no visible source of income, it was rumored that Zippy supported herself from a treasure-trove of coins that she had collected on the beach. When she died in 1884, her hut was supposedly invaded by a small horde of scavengers who hoped to find Zippy's treasure stash of coins—but none was found.

When the coastal road from Ocean City to Delaware was opened, the area where Zippy once lived had only a scattering of buildings near the beach. The new coastal road was a boon to motorists driving to Ocean City from Baltimore or Washington who wished to avoid the time-consuming ferry ride across the Chesapeake Bay by driving north around the head of the bay and down the coast. Three years later, the bridge across the Sinepuxent Bay was replaced with a higher, four-lane bridge that did not have to be opened as often and made both fishermen and motorists happier.

A MOVEABLE BEACH

While residents and visitors to the resort were dodging the traffic or looking for a place to park, someone was taking the Ocean City sand. The disappearance of the first grains went unreported, but by 1938, so many people noticed the steady erosion of one of the resort's greatest assets that a group of concerned citizens called on the city council to find out who was stealing Ocean City's beach. So much sand had been removed that Mayor Edmund Johnson predicted that when he looked as far as a million years into the future, he could see Ocean City as little more than a sea-swept knoll. The mayor, city council and the assembled town citizens all agreed that something had to be done about the vanishing Ocean City sand.

In the early days of the resort, there was little concern that Ocean City had too much sand, but in 1916, a bridge for cars and trucks was opened a short distance north of the railroad trestle. For the first time, cars and trucks could zip across the bay without fear of competition from an oncoming locomotive. While this made it easier for vacationers to reach the resort, it also made it easier for trucks to get out of town. During the prosperous 1920s, Ocean City was not the only town on the Eastern Shore that was booming. There were so many construction projects on the Delmarva Peninsula that contractors needed a dependable source of sand. The new bridge allowed the truckers to come to the resort, scoop up as much sand as they needed and head back to the mainland.

So much sand had been removed from the beaches that in 1927 an ordinance was passed that required truckers to deposit a load of mainland dirt for each load of Ocean City sand that they carted away. With the balance of soil maintained on the barrier island, the new ordnance seemed to alleviate the problems, and Ocean City sand was secure. In 1933, however, a hurricane struck and created the inlet. The storm also flooded the town's streets, and when the water receded, people began to assess the damage. As an eyewitness recalled, "The next day, the rain and wind stopped, and we got in the car to see the storm damage. We didn't get very far, only to Wicomico Street. Sand was everywhere."

With the streets inundated with sand, the town leaders encouraged truckers to cart the storm-driven stuff away. The 1927 ordinance was forgotten. As truckers removed the storm sand and returned the town to normal, the federal government initiated a series of construction programs to help combat the Great Depression. Truckers retuned to their former habits, and they drove over the bridge to load up on Ocean City sand.

After the town fathers put an end to the pilfering of one of Ocean City's finest assets, this young couple had plenty of sand to enjoy. *Courtesy of Carol Rechner.*

By 1938, the sand removal had reached crisis proportions. On December 7, a delegation of citizens met with the mayor and city council and demanded that something be done. As the city leaders pondered their next course of action. John M. Mumford, the city clerk, remembered the 1927 ordinance that required a deposit of a load of mainland soil per each load of sand that was to be trucked out of town. The town leaders agreed that the old law should be strictly enforced, and soon the steady parade of dump trucks that had been pilfering the resort's sand came to an end.

ENEMY OFF THE COAST

The summer of 1941 was a busy but ominous time in Ocean City. The Great Depression was over, and workers had plenty of money for a visit to the resort. On the other hand, Germany had attacked Poland in 1939, and the newspapers followed the war in Europe and the movements of Japanese forces in Asia. Following Labor Day, the resort settled down for its usual winter hibernation. On Sunday, December 7, 1941, many coastal families spent the afternoon gathered around the radio, where they were stunned by chilling words: "We interrupt this broadcast. The Japanese have bombed Pearl Harbor."

The Japanese surprise attack on Pearl Harbor plunged the United States into World War II, and in this conflict, Ocean City was unmistakably on the front lines. During the second week of January 1942, one of the army's small, single-engine planes was forced to land on the beach in front of the Coast Guard Station. One of three occupants of the aircraft was slightly injured, and the plane was quickly removed from the beach.

Off the coast, the German submarine *U-103*, commanded by Kapitanleutnant Werner Winter, was hunting for American ships. On February 2, Winter torpedoed the tanker *W.L. Steed*. Two days later, he sent the freighter *San Gil* and the tanker *India Arrow* to the bottom. Winter's success was repeated by other enemy U-boats, and the submarine attacks caused the captains of many merchant ships to sail close to the Maryland shore. One of these, the *Olaf Bergh*, was caught by a storm and driven onto the Ocean City beach. Until the hull was removed from the sand, huge crowds of sightseers flocked to the resort to see the stranded ship.

With enemy submarines prowling Ocean City waters, an appeal went out for volunteers to act as airplane spotters in Worcester County. Two months before Pearl Harbor, the Aircraft Warning Service (AWS) had been established to watch for enemy aircraft. When German submarines appeared off the coast, the fear that enemy aircraft would bomb coastal Maryland towns was never more real. Wearing a distinctive royal blue armband embroidered with the golden wings of the AWS, the volunteer observers had to know the difference between civilian and military aircraft,

An armband worn by a member of the Aircraft Warning Service, located at the Julia A. Purnell Museum in Snow Hill. *Photo by Michael Morgan.*

they had to distinguish a fighter from a bomber and they had to recognize a friendly plane from an enemy. To help train the AWS observers, the U.S. Air Force produced a variety of training aids, but the most effective was the use of scale model airplanes that could be viewed from a variety of angles and distances. To produce these models, kits were distributed to schools so that kids could build small replicas of American and enemy aircraft.

It was obvious to American authorities that the captains of German U-boats had learned to sit offshore and watch for American vessels as they were silhouetted by the lights of coastal communities. Eventually, blackout regulations were adopted that required those living in seaside towns to shield lights so that they would not shine out to sea. Cars approaching Ocean City were stopped by police, who instructed the drivers to use only their parking lights while in the resort. Streetlights were painted black on the seaward side, windows of buildings on the beach were equipped with blackout shades and light baffles were erected on doorways that opened toward the sea. To further minimize the light in the resort, two major streets were turned into one-way thoroughfares. Baltimore Avenue carried northbound traffic, and Philadelphia Avenue handled southbound cars. To ensure that these efforts were effective, blackout wardens patrolled the beach to watch for any lights that might shine out to sea.

In the early months of World War II, there was a great concern that spies might be lurking along the coast. Restrictions were placed on photographing and sketching the coast so that the details of the Maryland beach could not be used by an enemy planning an invasion. The fear of spies along the coast intensified in March, when the Federal Bureau of Investigation (FBI) arrested two enemy aliens. The arrests were the results of a series of raids conducted by federal and state agents in twenty-three communities on the Delmarva Peninsula. In addition to arresting the two men, the agents confiscated several swastika armbands, flags, four hundred rounds of ammunition, numerous rifles, short-wave radios, cameras and photographic developing equipment. The two men were hustled off to Baltimore for further questioning.

With the prospect of enemy U-boats offshore and spies lurking onshore, there seemed to be little hope that Ocean City could sustain a normal summer season. Mayor Clifford Cropper, Chamber of Commerce president Charles Purnell and other resort leaders proposed that the resort's hotel and housing facilities be made available to the federal government for use as a possible military base. The military forces had already leased hotels in Miami Beach, and Ocean City could accommodate more than fifteen thousand people. The federal government, however, declined the offer to turn Ocean City into a military base.

By the beginning of June, the situation in Ocean City had begun to brighten. The blackout regulations, the institution of the convoy system and vigilant surveillance of the Atlantic by military forces and civilian aircraft convinced the Germans to discontinue submarine warfare in America's coastal waters. During the summer of 1942, vacationers in Ocean City could look at the surf with the knowledge that the front lines of World War II had retreated to the other side of the Atlantic Ocean.

By the time that Memorial Day 1943 arrived, visitors to the beach had to contend with blackout regulations, gasoline rationing, travel restrictions and other wartime measures. Fewer than normal vacationers visited the resort for Memorial Day, but the first week of June was as busy as the previous year. By the time that the Fourth of July holiday arrived, Ocean City was on the way to having one of the most prosperous summers in a decade.

According to one hotel manager, "People are coming here for much longer stays than formerly. The one or two day visit is a thing of the past. We get fewer visitors, but they remain longer and spend far more." While moms stayed in the resort with the kids, dads took the bus back home and

Equipped with a captain's hat and shirt decorated with airplanes, this young beachgoer was nonetheless more interested in the sand than in the war. *Courtesy of Carol Rechner.*

returned to the resort every few weeks. This resulted in a more affluent, but subdued, crowd. One resort businessman remarked, "The old days when youngsters slept in their rattle-trap automobiles or under the boardwalk are gone. Now the young fellows are as well-heeled as the older people and they don't seem to mind spending."

The operator of a soda fountain and bowling alley noted that the reduction in overnight visitors hurt many of the bingo tables, shooting galleries and other amusements that were usually packed on weekends during the summer: "The concessions made their money on the overnight visitor. Young couples in their twenties used to drive here after work, have a meal, drink some beer, bowl a bit and drive home the next morning. Now children and mothers are in the majority."

As vacationers continued to crowd into the resort, proprietors of businesses in Ocean City snubbed their noses at state and county gambling laws. According to the *Baltimore Sun*:

> *The automobiles were rivaled in numbers only by the various types of slot machines which are operated in many a beer parlor, drugstores, restaurants and hotels in the resort…Gambling, in fact, is possibly the greatest attraction here, except for the beach, judging from the thousands of men, women and children found patronizing games of chance ranging from the innocuous "grab bag," in which one pays a dime, pulls a string and takes a chance on what prize he gets, to bingo, "pokerino" and the ubiquitous "one-armed bandits," which lap up nickels, dimes and quarters from one end of Ocean City to another.*

In addition to gambling, the resort also had an "anything goes" attitude toward alcohol. At that time, it was illegal in Worcester County to serve mixed drinks, and bottled liquor was supposed to be purchased at county-run dispensaries, but in Ocean City, clubs and beer parlors along the boardwalk openly sold mixed drinks. The resort's police chief, L.B. Cropper, admitted that "[w]e know its going on, but we don't have any evidence. We never go into those places unless we are called to quell a disturbance. The State's Attorney's office handles it. If we took action, we might interfere with the State's Attorney's efforts."

Although the resort may have winked at the gambling and alcohol laws, Ocean City could not escape the law of supply and demand that inflated many prices in the resort. Vacationers who arrived in the resort during the summer of 1943 discovered that prices had jumped dramatically since the war had begun. Beer was now $0.30 per bottle, and prices for mixed drinks began at $0.60. Prewar meals in many hotel dining rooms were a standard $1.00 per plate. Now they ranged from $1.50 to $2.00. In addition to the rising cost of food and drinks, hotels were charging as much as $10.00 for a single room. Thomas O'Donnell, writing in the *Baltimore Sun*, commented on the rising prices in the resort:

> *As an example of how prices have risen under war conditions, salt-water taffy which used to sell for twenty cents a pound now retails for eighty cents, and the only place selling home-made taffy is swamped with buyers and is sold out within twenty minutes each time it opens. This is the procedure: The place is closed all morning while the candy is being made. It opens around noon and almost immediately is sold out. Then it closes all afternoon while a new supply is being made and this is bought up later in the day.*

Those who managed to get enough gasoline to drive to the resort were not immune to the rising prices. At the time, a parking ticket in Baltimore cost the motorist $1.25, but drivers who parked illegally in Ocean City were fined an astounding $4.25. The high price of parking tickets did not deter some drivers who arrived for the Labor Day weekend. The resort resembled a vast parking lot, and many of the cars had the ubiquitous parking tickets neatly attached to their windshields.

Mayor Clifford P. Cropper was pleased that many businesses in the resort were having a successful summer, despite the wartime regulations: "We're making out mighty well despite all these difficulties. The beach is not rationed."

One of the biggest challenges faced by resort businessmen was the labor shortage caused by the war, but some proprietors discovered an unusual source of workers. Hotel operators kept a close watch on the town jail. Whenever cooks, elevator men, bellboys or other hotel workers were arrested for a minor offense, agents for the hotel owners competed for the privilege of paying the offender's fines. The released prisoner then went to work for his rescuer.

By the end of 1943, the labor situation on many Maryland farms had become critical. Some state leaders predicted that the lack of workers would cause the next crop to rot in the fields. Prisoners of war were being employed on some American farms, but Worcester County remained in the Vital Air Defense Zone of the Eastern Defense Command, and officials were reluctant to allow POWs in this important area. In February 1944, the security regulations were relaxed to allow the establishment of six POW camps on Maryland's Eastern Shore. A camp surrounded by double barbed wire fences, with searchlights and machine-gun towers at strategic points,

A captured German prisoner of war at work at an Eastern Shore orchard. *Courtesy of the Julia A. Purnell Museum.*

was established in Berlin near Route 50. Inside the wire fences were several wooden buildings and tents that held sleeping quarters for more than six hundred prisoners. In addition, the POW camp had a dining hall, washrooms and other facilities. Administrative offices, a small hospital area and quarters for the guards were built outside the fenced enclosure. Worcester County farmers and businessmen contracted with the War Food Administration of the Department of Agriculture for the use of prisoner of war labor. The captured soldiers were restricted to ten hours of work a day. They also could not be kept away from the camp in Berlin for more than twelve hours at a time. The POWs had an absolute right to a lunch break, and they were not to be abused or mistreated.

An American soldier stands guard while enemy prisoners of war work on the Eastern Shore. *Courtesy of the Julia A. Purnell Museum.*

To avoid undercutting the wages of American workers, contractors paid the prevailing civilian wage for POW labor. At that time, coastal workers made four dollars day; the prisoners usually received only eighty cents a day. The rest of the money was used to defray the cost of feeding and housing the prisoners.

By the time that the Berlin camp was established, Germany had been defeated, but most observers believed that the war in the Pacific would continue for another two years. In August 1945, the use of the atomic bomb brought the war against Japan to a quick end. After the surrender of Japan in August 1945, the POW camp at Berlin was disbanded, the blackout regulations were discontinued and families could look forward to pleasant Sunday afternoons listening to the radio and lounging on the beach.

CHAPTER 6

GOING DOWN THE OCEAN

THE GREAT GAMBLING RAID

In 1946, the end of World War II freed the resort from blackout regulations, and the lights were back on. As vacationers flooded into the resort during July, Sheriff Edwin Lynch met with half a dozen newly sworn deputies on the north edge of town. Lynch and his deputies were joined by six members of the Maryland State Police. Once the men had assembled and a large truck arrived, Lynch led the posse to Rick's Raft Club.

In 1946, Rick's Raft was one of the newest nightclubs in the resort. It was established and operated by Charles Rickards on Philadelphia Avenue between Sixteenth and Seventeenth Streets. At that time, there were few other buildings in the vicinity of the nightclub, which sat on the bay side of Philadelphia Avenue, half a dozen vacant blocks from the developed part of Ocean City.

In 1946, Ocean City tolerated activities that were frowned upon in the rest of Worcester County. At that time, it was illegal to sell mixed drinks in Worcester County, and gambling was also against the law, but many hotels had slot machines in their lobbies. The previous winter, the city had passed an ordinance that required a $150 tax from every person who owned, rented or leased any machine that could be operated for profit. The phrase "machine that could be operated for profit" was a local euphemism for slot machines, and it provided a convenient loophole for Ocean City gamblers. Resort authorities took the attitude that if no one was observed taking any winnings from a slot machine, then it could not be determined if it were being operated for profit. During the summer of 1945, Ocean City police conducted an inspection of more than four dozen resort businesses and reported that they did not see a single "machine that could be operated for profit." Nonetheless, slot machines were clearly visible in many businesses, and cash bingo remained a popular resort activity. In 1946, Worcester County sheriff Lynch's posse that descended on Rick's Raft Club did not include a single member of the Ocean City police force.

When Lynch's deputies entered the nightclub, they surprised a large group of people, but none was gambling. The deputies moved quickly to a back room, where they hit the jackpot. The room was crowded with gaming tables, slot machines and more than four dozen gamblers who were crowded around the dice games and high-stakes card games. As the police moved through the room, they snatched money from the tables and out of the hands of the surprised patrons. For a few minutes there was pandemonium as Lynch announced the people in the room were under arrest. While the police loaded the dice tables, slot machines and other gambling paraphernalia onto their truck, some of the people were able to slip away. Lynch agreed to release seventeen of those whom he had arrested provided that they post $50 for bail on the spot. Some quickly gave the sheriff the cash, and club owner Rickards stepped forward and posted the $50 for those who did not have it. Six others arrested by Lynch were considered principals in the gambling operation, and they were required to post a $500 bond. In addition to several thousand dollars in bond money, Lynch left Rick's Raft with more than $5,000 that his posse had scooped up from the tables and out of the hands of the gamblers.

The next morning, few people denied that there was gambling being conducted at Rick's Raft, but nearly everyone had something to say about the legality of the raid. Ocean City officials maintained that the state police could not enter the town unless the resort's authorities invited them. On the other hand, Sheriff Lynch contended that the nightclub was outside the town limits. The resort leaders countered that they had recently extended the boundaries of Ocean City to include Rick's Raft. A state official said that they had invited the resort police to participate in the raid but that Joseph Savage, Ocean City chief of police, said that he had been notified only fifteen minutes before the raid took place. At first, all of those arrested in the raid demanded jury trials, but a week later they agreed to plead guilty. Rickards and the six principals were fined $252.50 each; the seventeen patrons were fined $12.50. In addition, despite the protests of Sheriff Lynch, all of the money seized in the raid was returned.

While state, county and resort authorities argued over the legality of Lynch's raid and who said what to whom, most of the slot machines that had been clearly visible in Ocean City's clubs, hotels and stores disappeared. Bingo games began to reward winners with cigarettes instead of cash. Although gambling had been tolerated in the resort for some time, the raid on Rick's Raft demonstrated how elaborate some of the gambling operations had become. Some in the resort believed that gambling was attracting an undesirable element to Ocean City. A few days after the raid, Robert Lee Cropper, president of the Ocean City Chamber of Commerce, said that "[t]he big stuff must go…it becomes a racket and it has got to go." A month after the initial raid, Ocean City police made a second raid on Rick's Raft and another Ocean City night spot, but they found no evidence of gambling and no one was arrested. During the next few years, gambling would reappear in the resort, but it would never be as open as it was before Sheriff Edwin Lynch's midnight raid on Rick's Raft.

A BRIDGE TO THE FUTURE

While gamblers were trying their luck at Rick's Raft, Richard Hall was working on a sure thing. A native of Brooklyn, New York, Hall spent his boyhood summers in Worcester County, and at the end of World War II, he returned to the area, where he decided to try an idea that he had seen working on Long Island. With financial backing from I.I. Benjamin, a Salisbury merchant, Hall bought eleven blocks of bay-front property in 1946, and in the fall of that year, the roar of dredges along the Sinepuxent began drowning out the wild cry of the gulls. Mosquito-infested swampland was on its way toward becoming valuable real estate. He cut canals and lagoons in the swampy areas that bordered the coastal bay. After bulkheading the new waterways, he piled fill dirt onto the marshy ground until it was raised seven feet above sea level. With his reclaimed land ready for sail, all Hall needed was an influx of vacationers to fulfill his dream of an Ocean City where pleasure craft rode through his canals into the coastal bay.

When the suggestion to build a bridge across the Chesapeake Bay was first broached in the early twentieth century, it was dismissed as an expensive pipe dream. Following World War I, the State of Maryland began to modernize its roads, and in 1938 the Ritchie Highway was opened. Considered a showpiece of modern road construction, the Ritchie Highway enabled motorists from Baltimore to drive to the ferry landing outside Annapolis for the trip across the bay. Although the ferry took only forty-five minutes to cross the bay, the time spent waiting for the ferry to arrive and loading the cars added as much as four hours to the trip to Ocean City; in the year that the Ritchie Highway was opened, the Maryland General Assembly authorized the construction of a bridge across the bay. World War II began before construction could begin.

In 1940, Gerald W. Johnson wrote in the *Baltimore Evening Sun*:

> *Like all beaches that at Ocean City is subject to the vagaries of the winter storms; but as a usual thing there isn't a finer natural beach between Maine and Florida but getting to it, from Baltimore, is a really appalling job. The inevitable result is that a good many Marylanders visit beaches in Delaware and New Jersey that are not a whit better, but are more easily reached.*

The proposed bridge caused an uproar from many Eastern Shore residents who felt that their quiet way of life would be destroyed by an invasion of motorists. In addition, the bridge was attacked by maritime interests who felt that the structure would cause a serious hazard to navigation. When it was demonstrated that the ships could safely navigate past the bridge, some complained that the structure would remain a "mental hazard" to mariners. In the face of this opposition, the leaders of Ocean City lobbied hard for the project, and in 1949, work on the bridge began. After three years of construction, the new bridge was ready, and on July 30, 1952, a crowd estimated at twenty thousand people, plus Francis the Talking Mule, assembled for the opening of the span. During the dedication ceremony, led by Maryland governor Theodore R. McKeldin, former governor Preston Lane remarked, "The completion of the bridge marks the realization of a dream of over forty years. It is the most outstanding single accomplishment that Maryland has ever accomplished." It was now possible to drive from Baltimore to Ocean City in less than four hours.

The Chesapeake Bay Bridge sparked so much growth in Ocean City that within a few years the bridge was choked with traffic every summer weekend. Four years after the bay bridge was opened, modern concrete buildings began to be constructed in Ocean City, and these large boxy structures contrasted sharply with the older wooden buildings, with their peaked roofs and wide porches, that had dominated the resort since its inception. As one observer put it, "Maryland's only seaside resort [was turning] into a curious architectural blend that looks like a Florida boom town as well as an overgrown Eastern Shore fishing village."

Charles B. Harmon was a veteran motel builder when he came to Ocean City. Harmon had built motels on Route 1 between Baltimore and

During the 1950s, substantial houses were being built as far north as 143rd Street. *Courtesy of Linda Mitchell.*

Washington, three on Route 301, two in Salisbury and one in Pocomoke. In 1948, he opened a motel on the mainland opposite Ocean City, and with the Chesapeake Bay Bridge promising to bring a new flood of vacationers, Harmon began to build half a dozen motels in the resort. Other entrepreneurs quickly followed in Harmon's footsteps.

In 1956, Audrey Bishop commented in the *Baltimore Sun*:

> *Ocean City's largest motel—and also the largest modern one in Maryland—is new this season. It is a three story 111-room structure built on the boardwalk at Fifteenth Street by Mrs. Charles Ludlam, who has been in the hotel business for 47 years, much of the time in Ocean City. Most of the staff of Mrs. Ludlam's motel is made up of students in Cornell University's School of Hotel Administration. Every thing is becoming giant-sized in Ocean City, including the price of its real estate. Lots on Sinepuxent bay, which sold at auction for $600, now are tagged at $3,500.*

On both sides of the highway that connected Ocean City with Delaware, sand dunes and marshes were being replaced with motels, apartment houses and individual homes. Across Sinepuxent Bay, the road leading into town was being commercialized by the construction of motels, shops and other facilities. According to Bishop:

These vacationers were among those who flooded to the beach the year after the Chesapeake Bay Bridge was opened. *Courtesy of Carol Rechner.*

The motels that have sprouted northward along the Atlantic and back on the bay offer tourist accommodations of a sort that were unknown in Ocean City a few years ago—everything from air-condition and wall-to-wall carpeting inside, to swimming pools, barbecues and marines on the premises. In the older sections of Ocean city the "new look" is less pronounced. The barnlike frame structures that have been the resort's trademark still dominate the downtown skyline, but modern restaurants, shops, apartments, even a few motels, are now scattered among them.

When the Atlantic Hotel opened in the nineteenth century, visitors to Ocean City expected nothing more than the surf, the sand, a place to sleep and three good meals a day. And in most cases, that is what they got. For decades, many hotel rooms did not have rugs on the floors, innerspring mattresses on the beds or curtains on the windows. But after the Chesapeake Bay Bridge opened, the resort changed. New hotels featured air conditioning, wall-to-wall carpeting and swimming pools, and the owners of older establishments attempted to keep pace by sprucing up the exteriors of their buildings with modern façades to make them more attractive. In addition, hotel owners offered extras such as bathers' lunches, shuffleboard, clambakes and boat rides to attract guests. The live bands that once entertained vacationers at most hotels were replaced by television. The shadowy black-and-white pictures were often obscured by a blizzard of snow interference, but hotels guests crowded around the sets for a glimpse of their favorite programs.

The changes in Ocean City after World War II were so dramatic that it was hard to associate the new resort with the relaxed town that been hosting vacationers for so many years. As one hotel manager commented in the *Baltimore Sun*:

> *All of a sudden Ocean City was part of the rest of Maryland. The streets seemed to fill up overnight. The bridge not only opened Ocean City to Baltimore and Washington traffic, but it brought us business from out of State. We now draw people from Connecticut, New York, Virginia, Pennsylvania, and Ohio. Each year they seem to come from farther-away places. It's a far, far cry from the old days when motorists had to depend on the ferry to get across the Chesapeake.*

At that time, Ocean City officially ended at Twenty-sixth Street, and north of the resort, the road to Delaware passed through several miles of natural dunes that surrounded an occasional building. At the end of World

Two new buildings stood at Forty-fifth Street in 1954 as the resort expanded northward. *Courtesy of Carol Rechner.*

While the resort's leaders contemplated installing traffic signals, these two vacationers traveled the old-fashioned way. *Courtesy of Carol Rechner.*

War II, there were only 146 buildings between Fifteenth Street and Fenwick Island. After the Chesapeake Bay Bridge was opened, developers rushed to buy lots north of the resort, and a vast array of motels, restaurants and other buildings began to rise on the dunes. Audrey Bishop noted in the *Baltimore Sun*: "In short, Ocean City has become urbanized in such a hurry that pedestrians are finding it hard to buck the heavy traffic on the beach highway. Traffic lights are the obvious answer, and it's safe to guess that several will be installed before long."

While the town fathers contemplated adding traffic signals to regulate traffic on the resort's streets, construction continued north of the city. Between Ocean City and Delaware there were eight motels on the ocean side of Coastal Highway and twenty on the bay side. The building boom of the 1950s encouraged resort leaders to plan a new $7 million amusement pier that would contain swimming pools, shops, a skating rink, a sports arena, a theater, a convention hall, an aquarium, a heliport and radio and television stations. A new Ocean City was rising on the beach, but when the building boom began to dissipate, the plans for the grandiose pier were quietly forgotten.

Despite the town's growth, Ocean City continued to shut down during the winter months. On Monday morning, December 29, 1958, the resort was nearly deserted. On that chilly Monday, folks gathered around their television sets to watch *Father Knows Best*, *The Danny Thomas Show* and *Sugarfoot*. The newspapers carried reports that a showdown was near in the Cuban revolt. The rebel leader, Fidel Castro, was leading his troops on Santiago in what appeared to be the climactic battle of the two-year-old civil war. On the other hand, coastal sports fans were still regaling in the sudden-death overtime victory of the Baltimore Colts over the New York Giants for the National Football League championship. During the day, intermittent rain and a strong northeast wind kept Ocean City residents far from the beach, and it is doubtful that anyone noticed the tanker *African Queen* as it slowly made its way past the resort.

The *African Queen* was only three years old when it arrived off Ocean City. The 590-foot-long vessel was built in Germany, and the ship was used to carry crude oil from Cartagena, Colombia, to Paulsboro, New Jersey, on the Delaware River. The ship's cargo of 150,000 gallons of crude oil caused the vessel to ride low in the water, and the *African Queen* steamed relatively close to shore as it passed the resort. From the beach, the Atlantic Ocean appears to be a uniform expanse of deep water; but beneath the waves, offshore sandbars rise dangerously close to the water's surface. When loaded, the *African Queen* drew over thirty feet of water, and as the vessel steamed along the coast, the ship's keel was perilously close to the bottom.

Aboard the *African Queen*, Captain Kia Danielsen was having difficulty determining his exact position. The wind and rain had greatly reduced visibility, and he believed that he was close to the mouth of Delaware Bay. Danielsen ordered a turn to port in order to get a better look at the lights that would lead him around Cape Henlopen. The *African Queen*, however, was about thirty miles south of the cape. The turn brought the tanker on a collision course with the sandbars off Ocean City.

The impact of the *African Queen* striking the sand was hard to distinguish from the usual buffeting of the waves. The shock of the ship sliding onto the sandbar was so slight that it failed to awaken some of the sleeping crewmen, but the ship's bow had received a fatal blow. Captain Danielsen attempted to free the ship by reversing the tanker's engines. As the vessel backed away from the sandbar, a loud cracking noise echoed over the vessel. One by one, the steel plates on the vessel's port side had given way and opened a gash that ran down one side of the ship and under the vessel's bottom. The bow section of the *African Queen* had been nearly ripped from the rest of the vessel. The two sections were held together only by the hull plates on the ship's starboard side.

As Danielsen watched in disbelief, the bow began to peel back toward the rest of the *African Queen*. As thousands of gallons of crude oil spilled into the ocean, the bow section of the tanker slammed into the aft section of the ship. The sounds of the two parts of the ship clanging together startled the crewmen who had managed to sleep through the first few minutes of the disaster. The starboard plates had given way, and the two sections of the ship were completely detached as they banged together in the rough seas. Several of the seamen attempted to hang fenders between the two sections to keep the bow from battering the rest of the *African Queen* to pieces. After a few harrowing minutes, the two parts of the tanker began to drift apart.

All of the crewmen were aboard the aft section of the ship, which appeared to have the best chance for staying afloat. Moments after the *African Queen* had run onto the sandbar, a distress call was broadcast, and Coast Guard vessels from Cape May, Lewes and Ocean City responded. The strong wind and heavy waves made it impossible for the rescue vessel to pull alongside the aft section of the broken tanker. Helicopters were summoned, and all of those aboard the *African Queen* were plucked to safety. The crewmen were taken to the gymnasium of the Ocean City Elementary School at Baltimore Avenue and Third Street, where cots had been set up for them.

Officially abandoned by the ship's owners and crew, the two sections of the *African Queen* remained visible off Ocean City for some time. The front section was a total loss, and it settled on a sandbar, with its bow pointed toward the sky. The larger stern section of the ship was severely damaged, and it also settled on a sandbar, but it remained on an even keel. When the storm subsided, coastal watermen descended on the stern section, and they began to strip the vessel of anything of value. Lifeboats, paint, navigation equipment and other items were quickly ferried ashore.

For several weeks, sightseers visited the coast for a glimpse of the remains of the stranded tanker. Eventually, an enterprising group of salvagers managed to patch the stern section of the *African Queen*. After the tanker was towed to Norfolk, the winter beaches of Ocean City returned to their normally deserted condition.

In February 1960, two years after the *African Queen* broke up off the beach, Ocean City's winter residents were startled to find the beach covered with starfish. When Mayor High T. Cropper saw the creatures spread across the sand, he commented, "I have been here for 41 years and I have [never] seen anything like it." A storm that lingered off the coast for three days created onshore winds that had driven thousands of the creatures onto the sand. As the tide receded, the animals were left high and dry. According to Cropper, "The surf was just saturated with them. I was born and raised here, and I've talked to a lot of others here, but I've never seen them on the beach like that." Most of the beached starfish were concentrated on the sand north of Twenty-seventh Street, where there were few buildings. The starfish did not remain long, and only a few sightseers were able to get a glimpse of the mass of starfish before the next high tide washed the creatures back into the sea.

Storm of the Century

By the 1960s, memories of the 1933 storm that swept away the fishing camp and cut the inlet had faded, but occasional passing storms reminded coastal residents that a capricious sea was perched on the edge of the sand. In 1954, Hurricane Hazel passed west of Ocean City, and the resort was spared from the storm's high winds. Nonetheless, the unusually high tides induced by the storm caused considerable damage to the boardwalk and buildings in Ocean City. In the following year, the resort was battered by two hurricanes (Connie and Diane), but damage along the Maryland coast was relatively light. For the next ten years, the waters off Ocean City were relatively quiet, but then resort residents learned that hurricanes were not the only storms spawned by an angry Atlantic Ocean.

In the early 1960s, vacationers packed Ocean City, where owners of motels and hotels scrambled to expand to accommodate the ever growing demand for rooms. Not only did the boom in coastal construction continue its steady drive northward, but it also spread southward across the inlet to Assateague Island. In the late nineteenth century, when Ocean City was in its infancy, the Synepuxent Beach Company had proposed building a second resort on the island, but this failed to materialize. In the 1920s, developers proposed another resort named South Ocean City, but it, too, never advanced beyond the planning stage. By the end of World War II, Assateague was home to several small Coast Guard Stations and a few primitive hunting lodges when developers began to cast their eyes on the last and largest undeveloped beach between North Carolina and Massachusetts. At the same time, conservationists were looking for ways to preserve the natural beauty of the island. On the southern part of Assateague, the federal government had established the Chincoteague Wildlife Preserve on the Virginia end of the island. Although there were a number of attempts to turn the rest of the island into parkland, these proposals gained little traction.

With the increased development of Ocean City after the opening of the Chesapeake Bay Bridge, investors saw a grand opportunity on Assateague. A group led by Leon Ackerman of Silver Spring, Maryland, acquired fifteen miles of oceanfront land on the island, and he began to divide the area into streets and lots. The new seaside community was dubbed "Ocean Beach," and prospective buyers were ferried from the mainland across Sinepuxent Bay to view the prime oceanfront lots that were priced between $1,250 and $8,500. Offering all the benefits of Ocean City without the annoyance of the growing congestion of the resort, the developers sold eight thousand lots, and the success of the nascent resort temporarily stalled the interest in turning Assateague into a public park.

By 1960, several dozen houses connected by the island's single road dotted Assateague. Ocean Beach growth, however, was stymied by the issue that Ocean City had to overcome when the original Atlantic Hotel was built. With the creation of the inlet, there was no bridge across Sinepuxent Bay to Assateague, and property owners on the island banded together to find financing for a bridge to the mainland. The group was able to build a short causeway from the mainland into the coastal bay, but work stopped well short of the island.

As this was going on, Ackerman donated 540 acres of the island to the State of Maryland in the hope that the state would build a bridge to the island. As they worked to open Assateague to development, they were opposed by William E. Green, a blunt-talking advocate for maintaining the undeveloped nature of the island. In 1961, however, the Maryland state government authorized $1.5 million for the construction of a bridge from the mainland to the island. Assateague and the rest of the coastal region seemed poised for a long period of uninterrupted growth, but in March 1962, a nor'easter was born in the western Gulf of Mexico.

When a low-pressure system migrates to the Atlantic coast, the warm ocean water allows the system to strengthen as it churns slowly northward. The counterclockwise movement of the low-pressure system creates strong northeast winds off the ocean that batter the beach. The 1962 storm formed when three pressure systems combined. The storm stalled for two days a few miles off the Delmarva coast. As the northeast winds pounded the beach, the new moon brought in a spring tide. The combination of high tides and constant offshore winds were most destructive on March 7, which was Ash Wednesday—thus that lumbering nor'easter is now known as the "Ash Wednesday Storm."

Driven by hurricane-force winds, waves spilled over the dunes on Assateague Island and poured into the coastal bays. In a repeat of the 1933 storm, water in the coastal bay rose, and Assateague Island was caught between the high bay waters and the raging ocean surf. At the southern end of the island, the high waters were held in check by the Chincoteague causeway, and the bay waters continued to erode the Assateague sands. Eventually, the water breached the island in at least two locations to create two temporary inlets.

In Ocean City, the spring storm had destroyed or damaged hundreds of buildings. Large sections of the boardwalk had been ripped apart and sent floating through the town's flooded streets. At that time, the town limits of Ocean City had been pushed to Forty-first Street, but the building boom had spread development much farther northward. At Seventy-first Street, the storm breached the dunes and created a temporary inlet. Water as deep as four feet filled many of Ocean City's streets, and amphibious vehicles were called in to rescue many of the resort's residents.

When the wind stopped and the water receded, many buildings in the coastal resorts were in shambles. The streets were clogged with mounds of sand and piles of splintered buildings, broken furniture and other debris. With the opening of the summer season only a few months away, it appeared that the building boom along the coast was over.

From March to Memorial Day, hordes of workers swarmed over the coast from Lewes to Ocean City. The streets were cleaned, buildings were repaired and boardwalks were replaced. Some storm scars remained when the first

The 1962 storm swept much of the beach clean. *Courtesy of Linda Mitchell.*

After the 1962 storm, construction resumed as Ocean City expanded toward the Delaware line. *Courtesy of Linda Mitchell.*

vacationers arrived in June, but most of the resorts were back to normal. On Assateague Island, the damage done by the storm had a different result. The storm had shifted parts of the island's beach several hundred feet to the west, destroyed the island's only paved road and washed away most of the houses of Ocean Beach. With much of the island swept clean of development, the call for Assateague to be turned into a park increased. The State of Maryland acquired a tract of land on the northern tip of the park, and the federal government, led by Secretary of Interior Stewart Udall, acquired the rest of the island as part of an effort to preserve the nation's seacoasts. When the legislation creating Assateague Island National Seashore was passed, Udall declared that "a necklace of six national seashores had been placed around our country."

HIGH ROLLERS AND HIGH-RISES

The storm of 1962 may have washed some areas of the beach clean, but it did little to keep Bobby Baker from realizing one of his dreams. Born in Pickens, South Carolina, Baker was appointed a page in the United States

Senate when he was only fourteen years old. Within two years, Baker was the Senate's chief page, and in 1949, when Lyndon Johnson was elected to the Senate, Baker was on the Senate clerical staff. Baker latched onto Johnson and the two rose together. Baker became known as "Lyndon's boy." According to another Senate aide, "Bobby was the man you called. He knew who was drunk, who was out of town, who was unreachable. He knew who was against a bill and why, and he maybe knew how to approach a senator and get him to swing around. Bobby was it."

Baker combined his political knowhow with a variety of business ventures that included partnerships in a law firm, a travel agency, an insurance agency and a Howard Johnson motel. His prize venture, however, was the new Carousel motel on the Ocean City dunes at 117th Street. The building was under construction when the 1962 storm hit, but the damage was repaired and work continued. By July, Baker was ready to open, and he asked his political buddies from Washington to help him celebrate. On July 22, seven busloads of assorted celebrities and political operators traveled to the resort for the gala opening of the Carousel, a motel, according to one national, "[d]edicated to 'the advise-and-consent' set." Short-skirted waitresses staffed what was described as "the jazziest of Baker's business ventures."

The glitz of Baker and the Carousel did not last long. On November 8, 1963, *Life* magazine reported that "[t]he dread cry of scandal, bane of all establishments, burst like a bombshell across the Washington autumn. It associated the name of Bobby Baker…with an incredible mingling of high office, high influence and high living."

Stories of influence peddling, call girls and other irregularities led to a Senate hearing at which Gertrude "Trudy" Novak testified about Baker's money-handling practices. According to *Time*:

> *Bobby Baker tossed bundles of money about like so much laundry. Frequently, she said, she would stop by Baker's Capitol office to pick up sizable sums for the Carousel's operating expenses. It was always in cash. Once, she said, she found his desk stacked with nearly $15,000 in $100 bills. Baker himself rushed off to the Senate floor, leaving Trudy and his secretary to count out $13,300 for the motel.*

In the wake of the scandal, Baker resigned from his government position, and he was eventually found guilty of theft, fraud and income tax evasion. He was sentenced to three years in federal prison. Baker sold his interest

Bobby Baker's original Carousel motel is dwarfed by the surrounding high-rise condominiums. *Photo by Michael Morgan.*

in the Carousel, which had opened a new phase of development in the northern dunes of Ocean City.

While the ruckus over Bobby Baker and his motel was being played out, crowds of vacationers continued to clog the Chesapeake Bay Bridge, and in 1966, the Maryland General Assembly authorized the construction of a new parallel span. Six years later, vacationers began driving across a new, three-lane bridge. The prospect that millions of vacationers from the Washington-Baltimore area would have an easier time driving "down the ocean" sparked another building boom. By this time, Ocean City had extended its boundaries northward to the Delaware line, but except for the Carousel motel and a few other structures, the beach north of Sixty-second street was marked by long stretches of undeveloped dunes.

In 1965, the town of Ocean City annexed all of the land from north of the resort to the Delaware line. Water and sewer lines were built, and developers began to plan for buildings never before seen along the coast. In 1971, John Waley introduced a new form of resort ownership when he opened Ocean's City's first high-rise condominium, the Calypso. Waley's building was only six stories tall, but he was already at work on another building farther up the beach that was twice that height. When the High Point opened the next

Three girls relax during a day at the beach in the 1960s. *Courtesy of Linda Mitchell.*

year, the condo sold out in three months. During the next two and a half years, permits for more than 7,700 condo units were issued in Ocean City, and the Maryland resort, which had experienced periodic building surges that washed over the sands like the ocean waves, found itself in a real estate boom without parallel in the resort's history. Buyers eagerly succumbed to promoters' promises:

> *You can be the carefree owner of a home by the edge of the sea. No grass to cut. No traffic driving by. Just sweeping views of ocean and blue horizons from your private balcony…The quality and convenience of all-electric living with frost-free icemaker refrigerators, self cleaning ovens, disposals, dishwashers, and central heating. The security of modern construction and guarded swimming areas. The luxury of sound proofing, full carpeting and air conditioning. All this set at the ocean's edge with unobstructed bay and ocean views.*

Within a short time, a line of high-rise structures rose on the beach north of the new Route 90 Bridge that allowed motorists to bypass downtown Ocean City and enter the resort at Sixty-second Street.

The owners of the new condominiums enjoyed a home by the edge of the sea. *Photo by Michael Morgan.*

High-rise construction provided thousands of new condo owners with unobstructed bay and ocean views. *Photo by Michael Morgan.*

This young man caught these crabs from the pier behind his bayside condo. *Photo by Madelyn Morgan.*

In spite of these glittering promises, there were not enough buyers to go around. The building boom ended in a sea of foreclosures, and it was several years before all of the units were sold. The boom, however, had changed Ocean City yet again. In 1974, Carleton Jones, who had been an astute observer of the Maryland scene for many years, reported:

If it is not exactly Disneyland, it isn't Coney Island either; and anyone who has not crossed the Sandy Point bar and visited the area in three or four years is in for an awesome visual surprise. You swing off Route 50 into 113, slide across the Isle of Wight onto a wide, low slung bridge and over Assawoman Bay. Stretched out just to the left is a parade of a score of shattering new high-rises that have cost Maryland and Virginia lenders about $200 million. No matter what you have been told or who is going broke building the thing, it is a superb sight—the biggest optical bombola Maryland has achieved since they finished the first Bay bridge. It looks like the city of Dallas floating on the Great Salt Lake.

The seasonal village near the inlet had been transformed into a year-round resort where people could enjoy "[t]he ultimate experience in condominium living by the sea."

HARRY KELLEY BULLDOZES THE BEACH

It was not salt water but rather the sand of Ocean City that Harry Kelley had in his blood as he sat on a weathered bulldozer perched on the Ocean City beach. Born just after the end of World War I, Kelley grew up as his father, a member of the Coast Guard, chased rumrunners along the coast. In 1925, Harry's parents and Minnie Lynch built the Royalton hotel on the boardwalk at Eleventh Street. By the time Harry was a teenager, his mom, Ethel, had became famous for the sticky buns and other baked goods that she turned out of the Royalton's kitchen. By the 1930s, Harry was old enough to serve on the beach patrol, and in the booming years after World War II, Harry and his mom built the Beach Plaza hotel. However, a traffic accident cut her life short. By the time of her death, Harry had already entered local politics, and when he became mayor in 1970, he placed a full-sized picture of his mother in his office.

During his years as mayor, condo construction boomed and then burst, but Kelley remained a steadfast promoter of the resort. When the Organization of the Petroleum Exporting Countries (OPEC) oil embargo of 1974 caused gas shortages that threatened to prevent motorists from driving to Ocean City, Kelley quietly stockpiled gasoline and sold it to local stations so that vacationers could be sure of having enough fuel to return home. Proclaiming that the resort was only half a tank away, Kelley saw to it that Ocean City made it through the gas crisis of the 1970s, and he helped the resort develop a reputation for dependability that would serve it well in future gas shortages and rising prices.

After combating the gas shortage, Kelley mounted a bulldozer to restore the eroding Ocean City beaches. When a series of nor'easters carried away so much sand that the surf was lapping at the base of some of the new condominiums, the federal government fretted over a beach replenishment plan that promised to take years to implement. Fearing that some buildings might tumble, Kelley had a bulldozer brought to the beach; amid much fanfare, he personally pushed the first load of sand back out of the surf and onto the beach. Soon, he had a squad of bulldozers working along the surfline. While environmentalists complained that the bulldozers were doing more harm than good, Kelley kept his bulldozers rolling until a plan was devised that allowed for offshore sand to be pumped onto the beach.

By 1982, Kelley had been mayor of Ocean City for more than a decade, and he had acquired a reputation as a coarse but straight-talking politician. Promising that he would do for the state of Maryland what he had done for Ocean City, Kelley decided to run for governor. With little statewide experience, but with a name recognition that his flamboyant activities in Ocean City had earned him, Kelley picked a young, level-headed lawyer, L. Mark Vincent, as his running mate. Although Vincent was not well known, he had political experience working in the Baltimore area, and his smooth manner balanced the ticket nicely.

Unfortunately, Kelley and Vincent were unsuccessful in their bid for statewide office. Nonetheless, Kelley was reelected as mayor of the resort, and Vincent returned to political obscurity. When Kelley died in 1985, Ocean City condo construction had settled down, motorists had devised ways to find gas to get to the beach and a beach replenishment plan was well underway to keep the sands of the new resort in place. In honor of the man who personified the heart and soul of Ocean City, the Route 50 span over Sinepuxent Bay was renamed "Harry Kelley Bridge."

THE SWEET SCENT OF OCEAN PINES

In the seventeenth century, when the first Europeans were moving into the Ocean City area, Colonel William Stevens, a confidant to Lord Baltimore, was busy acquiring land west of the coastal bays. He was looking for well-drained land that was close to navigable water. Although the coastal bays are not deep, Stevens knew that he could grow tobacco and other crops that he could float across the bay to Sinepuxent Inlet, where they could be loaded onto ships for more distant markets. Eventually, Stevens acquired more than twenty-six thousand acres of land between the Pocomoke River and the ocean, and he used the land to entice others to settle in the coastal region. After Stevens sold a parcel known as the Buckland Plantation to Colonel Francis Jenkins, the area became known as Jenkins Neck. As the years passed, part of the land, including an old farm known as Malvern, was acquired by Harry Selby Purnell, whose wife's family had lived on the farm for nine generations.

In the early twentieth century, a farmer who lived on the northern edge of the Buckland Plantation slaughtered hogs there and propped up the skulls

With the start of construction at Ocean Pines, the Ocean City area began a new phase of development. *Courtesy of the Ocean Pines Association.*

on the edge his property; the locale became known as the "Hog Skull" area. In 1968, Maryland Marine Properties, a subsidiary of Boise Cascade, began buying more than two dozen properties on the western shore of the coastal bay north of Riddle Farm. Among the tracts that the firm acquired were the Buckland property, Hog's Skull farm and Malvern, which was then owned by Harry Purnell's son, Franklin. In 1952, Franklin, who was a schoolteacher, borrowed $25,000 to buy his interest in the land from his mother. Sixteen years later, Purnell sold the farm to Maryland Marine Properties for $2 million and retired from teaching.

Situated on the St. Martin's River and astride the new Route 90 that led directly to Ocean City, the tract that Maryland Marine Properties had assembled included a trailer park, a pig farm, chicken farms, orchards, woods and farmland. In 1968, the sprawling property on the western shore of the coastal bay was rezoned to residential and commercial use, and the development of Ocean Pines was born.

With a vista of the rising skyline of Ocean City, the land was platted into lots, with streets laid out to preserve its rural character. A golf course was constructed, and along the edge of the bay, canals were dug so that Ocean Pines residents could enjoy waterfront living. In addition, a marina was built, and a lot on the oceanfront at Forty-ninth and Fiftieth Streets was developed into a beach club. After a sales office was established near the southern end of the Ocean City boardwalk, prospective buyers were ferried across the bay

The bayside development of Ocean Pines gave residents of the Ocean City area a new way of living. *Courtesy of the Ocean Pines Association.*

to the new development. In addition, an English double-decker bus was used to bring customers to Ocean Pines, which quickly became a permanent part of the Ocean City landscape.

ALL I WAS DOING WAS MY JOB

"Yes, I can swim." And with that, seventeen-year-old Bob Craig became a member of the Ocean City Beach Patrol. With the steady growth of Ocean City during the Roaring Twenties, devotees of the surf moved northward, and many were plunging into the ocean well past the sight of the Coast Guardsmen at Caroline Street. By the 1930s, several thousand vacationers were enjoying a dip in the ocean every day, and they were no longer wearing the confining suits worn by earlier beach visitors. Both men and women were wearing short, form-fitting suits that allowed for easier swimming, and many vacationers were no longer hanging on to the safety lines that enabled novice beachgoers to enjoy the surf. The dangers of a splash in the ocean had been part of the resort since its founding. In 1880, the *New York Times* reported what may have been the first drowning death at the resort, concerning "a day made memorable here by the death, by drown, of Senator Fords, of Queen Anne County, who, at the cost of his own life, saved a young lady from that death."

Knowing the perils that swimmers faced, Mayor William W. McCabe and Captain William Purnell of the Coast Guard organized the beach patrol, and Edward Lee Carey was hired to watch over the beach. A few years later in 1935, Bob Craig declared that he could swim. Armed with a small buoy and smelling salts, dressed in his own swim trunks and carrying his own towel, Craig began a fifty-two-year career in the beach patrol.

Craig was born and raised in Wilmington, Delaware, where his father was a schoolteacher. The Craig family spent the summers in a cottage in Ocean City, where he joined the budding beach patrol. After attending college and graduate school, Craig followed in his father's footsteps and became a teacher. At the end of World War II, he returned to Ocean City, where he was promoted to captain of the beach patrol, a position that he held for forty years. He once described himself as "[p]robably the longest-term employee the city has ever had."

At one time, a test for applicants to become members of the patrol involved rescuing Craig as he played the role of a distressed swimmer. Now, more systematic tests are conducted before the start of the vacation season, when the ocean water still retains its winter chill. Even today, two core elements remain from the test that Craig developed. Applicants must complete an ocean swim from the inlet jetty around the pier to the beach in ten minutes. Those who complete this swim, and most do not, must complete a daylong series of physical tests that include simulated rescues, running a 330-yard course in soft sand in under sixty-six seconds and fending off a panicked swimmer.

Those who are accepted are taught the semaphore signals, first aid and CPR training. In addition, patrol members learn about rip currents and how winds and tides will affect surf mats. Patrol members must also be skilled in dealing with a variety of people and situations. Although their primary mission is to maintain a safe beach environment by preventing deaths and injuries, patrol members also provide the public with information. During the season, they answer countless questions while watching swimmers and enforcing the rules of the beach that prohibit alcoholic beverages, glass containers, ball-playing, dogs and loud music. Sometimes this means dispensing a little common sense—like telling vacationers who would never let their children play with a dead squirrel not to let their kids play with a dead crab that may be laced with bacteria.

A member of the beach patrol uses semaphore to send a message the old-fashioned way. *Photo by Michael Morgan.*

Inspired by the late Bob Craig, an ever vigilant member of the Ocean City Beach Patrol stands guard. *Photo by Michael Morgan.*

When a swimmer gets into trouble, and members of the beach patrol dash toward the surf, they never know what they will encounter when they enter the waves. Jellyfish may be floating in the rescuer's path, and schools of biting bluefish can get in the way—but these hazards cannot deter the lifesaver. Captain Craig once estimated that in a typical season, the patrol goes to the rescue of more than three thousand bathers, handles several hundred lost children and is called on for first aid nearly two thousand times. Craig also once said that "a guard needs maturity to be able to tell someone as old as his grandfather that he is breaking the law."

When members of the beach patrol pull an exhausted swimmer from the surf, they never know what to expect. Craig once saw a near-drowning victim slap the guard who pulled her from the surf. On the other hand, a former member of the patrol recalled:

> *I had one man that I saved who was an active drowner. When I got to him I didn't think he spoke English since he wasn't responding to me verbally but was thrashing about…I got him on the beach, calmed him down, he walked away. The next day he came back and brought his wife who was also on the scene. She could not stop crying when thanking me. The next weekend the family came back again with their adult son who brought his children who wanted to meet me and thank me, give me money. All I was doing was my job.*

OC TODAY

On the north side of 146th Street, a weathered stone marker sits in the shadow of the Fenwick Island Lighthouse. When Maryland was established in the seventeenth century by George Calvert, the first Lord Baltimore, the borders of his new colony were poorly defined, and this led to a protracted dispute with William Penn and his family, who owned Pennsylvania and Delaware. After a general agreement on the borders of Maryland and its neighbors was reached, a surveying team arrived on the beach in December 1750 to precisely mark the boundary. As they worked, the surveyors marked the border with a series of stones incised with the coat of arms of the Penns on the north side and the coat of arms of the Calverts on the south side.

After another legal dispute suspended the work of marking the borders of Delaware for several years, Charles Mason and Jeremiah Dixon were hired to finish the work that had been started in 1750. In addition to the border between Maryland and Delaware, Mason and Dixon also surveyed the border between Maryland and Pennsylvania. When Pennsylvania abolished slavery, the border between Maryland and Pennsylvania became the nominal boundary between the North and the South. Today, the boundary stone on 146th Street denotes the border between Ocean City and the town of Fenwick Island, Delaware.

A block north of the boundary stone, Route 54 leads inland from Fenwick Island and serves as a third gateway to Ocean City. The road follows the route that Zippy Lewis took in the nineteenth century when she scavenged the beach and watched for the return of her husband. The dunes that she once frequented are now covered with condominiums and beach houses. On the bay side, the marshes have been filled and bulkheaded to create the firm ground for the houses of Caine Woods. Although the streets of this residential community are but a few blocks from the heavy traffic on Coastal Highway, during the busiest weeks of the summer season, the streets of Caine Woods are quiet.

South of Caine Woods, Bobby Baker's Carousel motel still faces the ocean, although the political operative's name is no longer associated with the building. Overshadowed by the large condominium tower that was built a decade after Baker opened his motel, the Carousel Hotel and

High-rises crowd the beach where Zippy Lewis once scavenged the sand for shipwreck debris. *Courtesy of the Delaware Public Archives.*

Condominiums retains a pleasant view of the beach and offers amenities that Baker could only have dreamed of when his political friends dedicated the original building.

At the Route 90 Bridge, cars stream into the resort as they pass through Ocean Pines, which has matured into a year-round community while still retaining much of its rural flavor. On the edge of the bay, the yacht club is filled with boats, and low-rise condos look eastward across the bay to the skyline of Ocean City. Not far from Ocean Pines, St. Martin's Church stands in a wooded grove by the side of Route 113.

South of the Route 90 Bridge in Ocean City, the string of condos and hotels continues to the inlet. On the bay side, restaurants, beach shops, retail areas, amusement areas, miniature golf courses and the resort's convention center compete for space with the houses, condos and motels. Just south of Twenty-first Street, Phillips Crab House stands in an area that half a century ago was on the northern edge of the resort.

In 1956, Shirley and Brice Phillips came to town and opened a small crab carry-out shop to sell the surplus supply of crabs and crabmeat from the family's seafood packing plant on Hooper's Island. The demand for their crabs was so great that the Phillips added a dining room to the original four-seat carry-out shack. Over the years, the popularity of Phillips continued to grow, and the family opened several other restaurants in Ocean City,

As they have done for more than a century, vacationers enjoy an early morning bike ride on the boardwalk. *Photo by Michael Morgan.*

Baltimore, Myrtle Beach and elsewhere. Today, the company that began as a small crab shack in Ocean City is among the most popular and largest-grossing family restaurant chains in the country.

In the southern part of town, Ocean City retains many of the buildings that were constructed in the early years of the twentieth century. The streets are lined with large homes and rooming houses, with their characteristic peaked roofs and wide porches. On the boardwalk, modern shops and restaurants obscure some of the original façades, but the upper stories of old Ocean City still loom over the steady parade of walkers. The pier and its amusements still thrust out into the ocean, while on the landward side the pier pavilion and the Atlantic Hotel—built after the 1925 fire—are visible behind the modern storefronts. In addition, Trimper's carousel still carries happy riders for a whirl on a colorful collection of animals.

Vacationers continue to crowd the Ocean City boardwalk. *Photo by Michael Morgan.*

The Ocean City pier and its amusements extend across the wide sand and into the ocean. *Photo by Michael Morgan.*

At the very end of the boardwalk, the Ocean City Life-Saving Station stands overlooking the inlet. Moved from its original location at Caroline Street, the building has been preserved as a museum of the history of the town. The station looks across the wide expanse of sand that has accumulated north of the stone groin that was built to stabilize the inlet. During the predawn hours of a midsummer morning, crowds gather along the inlet to watch the hundreds of fishing boats churn through the inlet on their way to Jackspot and other favorite fishing grounds as part of the annual White Marlin Open. The fishing tournament is one of the most popular in the country and has helped to make Ocean City the "White Marlin Capital of the World."

West of the inlet, Ocean City Harbor has become home port for many commercial and recreational fishermen. In recent years, development has spilled over the Route 50 Bridge into West Ocean City. Riddle Farm, where Man o' War once romped, has become an upscale real estate development with golf courses that retain architecture reminiscent of the time when the world's greatest thoroughbred lived by the beach. The developers have erected a tasteful arch that serves as a memorial to the world's greatest thoroughbred. A few miles away in Berlin, the red brick Atlantic Hotel has

The Ocean City Life-Saving Museum is the repository for a wide collection of artifacts and memorabilia associated with the history of the resort. *Photo by Michael Morgan.*

Each summer, the herd of ponies at the Virginia end of Assateague Island is driven across the channel to Chincoteague. *Photo by Michael Morgan.*

Even some of the youngest ponies make the swim from Assateague Island. *Photo by Michael Morgan.*

Glimmering in the twilight, Ocean City remains a sort of paradise. *Courtesy of the Ocean Pines Association.*

148

been restored, and it has been featured in several movies, including *Runaway Bride* with Richard Gere and Julia Roberts.

South of the inlet, the northern tip of Assateague Island has been seriously eroded by the wind and waves. Occasionally, the wild ponies can be seen from the south end of the boardwalk, but more often vacationers will take the short drive south over the Verrazano Bridge to visit Assateague Island. At the state and national parks on the island, visitors watch the wild ponies roam free, swim on a natural beach and see the wreckage of long-lost ships in the sand. In addition to the wild ponies, more than a hundred species of geese, osprey and other birds also inhabit Assateague Island, where it is not difficult to experience what it was like when Verrazano first visited the beach.

When vacationers finish their visits to Assateague and Ocean City, they make the long ride back across the Chesapeake Bay Bridge and go home. There they spend the winter months awaiting the familiar words.

"What are you going to do this summer, hon?"

"I am going down the ocean."

BIBLIOGRAPHY

Baltimore News-American. "Ocean City Savings During the Fall." August 19, 1973.

Baltimore Sun. "45,000 Flock to Ocean City for Labor Day." September 7, 1943.

———. "J.B. Lynch Quits Ocean City Post." August 10, 1946.

———. "Md. Resort Open 62 Years Today." July 4, 1937.

———. "Ocean City Asks U.S. to Lease Resort." May 22, 1942.

———. "Ocean City Frivolity Unhalted By Dim-Out." June 1, 1942.

———. "Ocean City Reservations at Peak." March 16, 1945.

———. "Paradox in Prices and Rates in Ocean City." July 25, 1945.

———. "Prices at Ocean City Disgust Traveler from Abroad, Jersey." July 31, 1946.

———. "Whiling Away the Summer at a Popular Maryland Resort." August 7, 1894.

———. "Yes, We've No Slot Machines." July 15, 1945.

Baker, E.T. "Ban on Pleasure Driving Proves Blow to Ocean City." *Baltimore Sun*, May 31, 1943.

Beachcomber. "The Storm of '33." Special Section, August 19, 1983.

Bishop, Audrey. "The New Look in Ocean City." *Baltimore Sun*, July 1, 1958.

Bittof, Mrs. N.H. "I Remember…A Much Different Ocean City." *Sunday Sun Magazine*, June 5, 1966.

Board of Commissioners of Worcester County. *Articles for Consideration: 250 Years of History, Worcester County, Maryland, 1742–1992*. N.p.: Board of Commissioners of Worcester County, 1993.

Brown, Nona. "More Vacationists for the Delmarva Seashore." *New York Times*, August 3, 1952.

Burch, Alisa. "Passing of Purnell Patriarch Recalls Early OC History." *Beachcomber*, March 16, 1984.

Carter, Richard B. *Clearing New Ground: The Life of John G. Townsend Jr.* Wilmington: Delaware Heritage Press, 2001.

Charles, Joan. *Mid-Atlantic Shipwreck Accounts to 1899.* Hampton, VA: self-published, 1997.

Chincoteague Island Chronicle. "The Legend Continues." *Chronicle* special edition, July 31, 1986.

Corddry, Mary. *City on the Sand: Ocean City Maryland and the People Who Built It.* Centreville, MD: Tidewater Publishers, 1991.

Cordingly, David. *Under the Black Flag.* San Diego, CA: Harcourt Brace & Company, 1997.

Cox, S.S. "The Life Saving Service." *North American Review* (May 1881).

Defoe, Daniel. *A General History of the Pyrates.* Ed. Manuel Schonhorn. Mineola, NY: Dover Publications, Inc., 1972.

Doughty, Frances Albert. "Life at a Life-Saving Station." *Catholic World* 65, no. 388 (July 1897).

Eastern Shore Times. "History of Resort Told by Resident." March, 24, 1936.

———. "Sea Captain's Grave Attracts Visitors; Wrecked in 1799." *Vacation News* section, 1941.

Folks, Kenneth Patrick. "I Remember the Wonderful Ocean City Flyer." *Baltimore Sun*, October 5, 1952.

Gentile, Gary. *Shipwrecks of Delaware and Maryland.* Philadelphia, PA: Gary Gentile Productions, 1990.

Hall, Richard. "Axis Prisoners of War in the Free State, 1943–1946." *Maryland Historical Magazine* 83, no. 2 (Summer 1988).

Harr, Dorothy N. *The Story of a Lost Village: Furnace Town.* Snow Hill, MD: Furnace Town Foundation, 1983.

Harris, Allen Will. "Ocean City Prepares for Fourth Throngs." *Baltimore Sun*, July 2, 1943.

Harrison, Sandra. *A History of Worcester County, Maryland.* Berlin, MD: Mayor and Council of Berlin, 1964.

Hayman, John C. *Rails Along the Chesapeake: A History of Railroading on the Delmarva Peninsula, 1827–1978.* Pittsburgh, PA: Marvadel Publishers, 1979.

Heland, Victoria J. *Worcester Memoires, 1890–1933.* Snow Hill, MD: Worcester Heritage Committee, 1984.

Henry, Frank. "Sand of Time—Ocean City." *Baltimore Sun*, July 5, 1953.

Hurley, George, and Suzanne Hurley. *Ocean City: A Pictorial History.* Virginia Beach, VA: Donning Company, 1979.

———. *Shipwrecks and Rescues Along the Barrier Islands of Delaware, Maryland, and Virginia.* Virginia Beach, VA: Donning Company, 1984.

Johnson, Gerald W. "A Road to Ocean City." *Baltimore Evening Sun*, February 15, 1940.

Jones, Carlton. "Across the Bay Bridge and into the Breeze." *Baltimore Sun*, June 2, 1974.

Keesey, Lori. "Recollections of Ocean City." *Maryland Magazine* (Summer 1996).

Keiper, Ronald. *The Assateague Ponies.* Centreville, MD: Tidewater Publishers, 1985.

Klein, Dan. "Questing for History." *Maryland Times-Press*, November 3, 1999.

Knott, Rota, L. "The Grand Old Hotels of An Era Gone By." *Entertainer Magazine* (July 1996).

Kotlowski, Dean. "The Last Lonely Shore: Nature, Man, and the Making of Assateague Island National Seashore." *Maryland Historical Magazine* 99, no. 2 (Summer 2004).

Lawson, John D., ed. *American Sate Trials.* Vol. 4. St. Louis: F.H. Thomas Law Book Company, 1915.

Lencek, Lena, and Gideon Bosker. *The Beach: The History of Paradise on Earth.* New York: Viking, Penguin Group, Penguin Putnam Inc., 1998.

Lewis, Sara. "Sailing at Ocean City." *Heartland of Del-Mar-Va* 11, no. 4 (Sunshine 1988).

Little Owl (Charles C. Clark IV). "The Nanticoke." *Heartland of Del-Mar-Va* 11, no. 4 (Sunshine 1987).

Long, David James. "Salt Mines of Fenwick Profitable Del. Venture." *Delaware News*, July 7, 1938.

Mackintosh, Barry. *Assateague Island National Seashore: An Administrative History.* Washington, D.C.: National Park Service, Department of the Interior, 1982.

Marye, William B. "The Sea Coast of Maryland." *Maryland Historical Magazine* 40, no. 2 (June 1945).

Maryland Coast Dispatch. "Ocean City for Sale." February 9, 1990, reprinted from the *Salisbury Advertiser*, February 20, 1897.

Maryland Coast Press. "Kelley Introduces His Running Mate." June 23, 1982.

Matthews, Katie Gaskings, and William Russell. *Worcester County: A Pictorial History.* Norfolk, VA: Donning Company, 1985.

McBee, Avery. "Ocean City Standing By for Summer Population." *Sunday Sun Magazine*, May 15, 1938.

McManus, James K. "'Maybe Best Year': It's Spring in Ocean City." *Baltimore Sun*, April 21, 1947.

Mellinger, Brandi. "Berlin's Riddle Farm, Once Home to Man o' War." *Maryland Times-Press*, October 10, 1992.

Mills, Eric. *Chesapeake Rumrunners of the Roaring Twenties*. Centreville, MD: Tidewater Publishers, 2000.

Moale, H. Richard. *Notebook on Shipwrecks on the Maryland-Delaware Coast*. Westminster, MD: Family Line Publications, 1990.

Morison, Samuel Eliot. *The European Discovery of America: The Northern Voyages*. New York: Oxford University Press, 1971.

Mullin, Gerald W. *Flight and Rebellion*. New York: Oxford University Press, 1972.

Murphy, Henry C. *The Voyages of Verrazzano*. New York, 1875.

New York Times. "Ambitious Plans for Man o' War." January 20, 1920.

———. "Destroyer Sights U-Boat." June 5, 1918.

———. "The Home of the Wild Duck." January 10, 1875.

———. "Man o' War First in the Preakness." May 19, 1920.

———. "Man o' War Heads Fine Field at Spa." August 3, 1918.

———. "Man o' War Takes Grand Union Hotel Stakes, with Upset Second." August 24, 1919.

———. "Maryland's Seaside Resort." April 1, 1880.

———. "Maryland Town Fire-Swept." October 2, 1904.

———. "Oysters in Synapuxant Bay." March 28, 1884.

———. "Sanford Memorial Is Won by Upset." August 14, 1919.

———. "Steamer *Saetia* Sunk by Mine." November 10, 1918.

———. "World Record Is Set by Man o' War." June 13, 1920.

Nicol, John, and Frederick C. Beach, eds. *The American Amateur Photographer*. Vol. 13. *January–December, 1901*. New York: American Photo Publishing Co., 1901.

Noble, Dennis L. *That Others Might Live: The U.S. Life-Saving Service, 1878–1915*. Annapolis, MD: Naval Institute Press, 1994.

Ocean Centennial Committee. *A Century of Seashore Hospitality: The History of Ocean City, Md*. Ocean City, MD: Ocean Centennial Committee, 1975.

Ocean Pines Progress 6, no. 2. "Passing of the 'Mother of Mumford's Landing' Recalls Memories of a Time before Ocean Pines" (August 2010).

O'Donnell, Thomas J. "Lid Clamped on Ocean City." *Baltimore Sun*, July 18, 1945.

————. "Night-Club Owner Prays Jury Trial." *Baltimore Sun*, July 24, 1946.

————. "Ocean City Plans Gambling Parley." *Baltimore Sun*, July 21, 1946.

————. "24 Men Fined in Ocean City." *Baltimore Sun*, July 25, 1946.

————. "Warrants Issued for Patrons, Principals in Ocean City Raid." *Baltimore Sun*, July 21, 1946.

Palko, Stephanie. "Public Landing, Worcester County's Former Most Popular Resort." *Beachcomber*, February 19, 1982.

Parkman, Francis. "The Acadian Tragedy." *Harper's New Monthly Magazine* 69, no. 414 (November 1884).

Passenger Department, Philadelphia, Wilmington and Baltimore Railroad. *A Paradise for Gunners and Anglers*. Philadelphia: Philadelphia, Wilmington and Baltimore Railroad Company, 1883.

Pohuski, Michael. "A U-Boat in Baltimore Harbor: The *Deutschland*, 1916–1921." *Maryland Historical Magazine* 87, no. 1 (Spring 1992).

Purnell, R. Franklin to Paul Plamann, personal letter, May 21, 1985.

Ritchie, Robert C. *Captain Kidd and the War against the Pirates*. New York: Barnes and Noble, 2006.

Rogner, Bud. *History of Ocean Pines, 30th Anniversary Edition, 1968–1998*. Showell, MD: Dearengor Co., 1998.

Salisbury Times. "FBI Arrests Two Aliens on Shore." March 14, 1942.

Scisco, Louis Dow. "Norwood in Worcester County in 1650." *Maryland Historical Magazine* 18, no. 2 (June 1923).

Shanks, Ralph, and Wick York. *The U.S. Life-Saving Service: Heroes, Rescues and Architecture of the Early Coast Guard*. Petaluma, CA: Costano Books, 1998.

Sheppeck, Mary Ellen Mumford. *A History of Ocean City Maryland*. Berlin, MD: Mayor and City Council of Ocean City, 1964.

Sherry, Frank. *Raiders and Rebels: The Golden Age of Piracy*. New York: Hearst Marine Books, 1986.

Shields, Jerry. *Gath's Literary Work and Folk*. Wilmington: Delaware Heritage Press, 1996.

Shomette, Donald G. *Pirates on the Chesapeake*. Centreville, MD: Tidewater Publishers, 1985.

Small, Clara L., and David Briddell. *"Man of Color, to Arms!" Manumitted Slaves and Freed Blacks from the Lower Eastern Shore of Maryland Who Served in the Civil War*. Fruitland, MD: Arcadia Enterprises, Inc., 2010.

Sollers, Basil. "The Acadians (French Neutrals) Transported to Maryland." *Maryland Historical Magazine* 3, no. 1 (March 1908).

Straw, Jennifer. "Historic St. Martin's Church Set for Turn-of-the-Century Debut." *Maryland Times-Press*, May 28, 1997.

Swanson, John Sr. "An Old 'Salt' Remembers Ocean City." *Entertainer*, May 1985.

Thompson, Neal. "Spending Time Saving Lives." *Baltimore Sun*, June 15, 2000.

Touart, Paul Baker. *Along the Seaboard Side: The Architectural History of Worcester County, Maryland*. Snow Hill, MD: Worcester County Commissioners, 1994.

Townsend, George Alfred. *The Entailed Hat*. Ed. Hal Roth. Vienna, MD: Nanticoke Books, 2000.

Truitt, Reginald V. *Assateague...the "Place Across": A Saga of Assateague Island*. College Park: University of Maryland Press, 1971.

Truitt, Reginald V., and Millard G. Les Callette. *Worcester County: Maryland's Arcadia*. Snow Hill, MD: Worcester County Historical Society, 1977.

Tucker, Glenn. *Dawn Like Thunder: The Barbary Wars and the Birth of the U.S. Navy*. New York: Bobbs-Merrill Company, 1963.

U.S. Department of the Interior. *Assateague Island National Seashore, Maryland Virginia, Handbook 106*. Washington, D.C.: U.S. Department of the Interior, 1980.

U.S. Life-Saving Service. *Annual Reports of the Operations of the United States Life-Saving Service*. Washington, D.C.: Government Printing Office, 1889–1913.

War of the Rebellion: A Compilation of the Official Records of the Union and Confederate Armies. 128 vols. Washington, D.C.: Government Printing Office, 1888–1901.

Warren, T. Robinson. "Bay Shooting." *Scribner's Monthly*, December 1876.

Willcox, Mrs. Edward. "I Remember Ocean City." *Sunday Sun Magazine*, May 29, 1960.

Wood, Gregory. *The French Presence in Maryland, 1524–1800*. Baltimore, MD: Gateway Press, Inc., 1978.

Wroten, William H. Jr., *Assateague*. Centreville, MD: Tidewater Publishers, 1981.

Young, Luther. "At 93, He Has Ocean of Memories of O.C." *Baltimore Sun*, August 8, 1985.

Websites

Archives of Maryland Online, vols. 16 and 28. http://aomol.net/html/index.html.

Callander, Bruce D. "The Ground Observer Corps." *Air Force Magazine* 89, no. 2 (February 2006). http://www.airforce-magazine.com/MagazineArchive/Pages/2006/February%202006/0206goc.aspx.

Craig, Robert, Captain, Ocean City Beach Patrol, Maryland. "OC Family Grateful." *Maryland Coast Dispatch*, May 25, 2009. http://www.freerepublic.com/focus/chat/2257938/posts.

Hurley, Suzanne B. "Captain William Carhart." Ocean City Life-Saving Museum. The Times & Tides of Ocean City, Maryland, 1991. http://www.ocmuseum.org/index.php/site/oc-history_article/captain_william_carhart.

Lee, Skip, First Lieutenant. "Ocean City Beach Patrol." Town of Ocean City. http://oceancitymd.gov/Recreation_and_Parks/Beach_Patrol/history.html.

Norwood, Henry, Colonel. *A Voyage to Virginia*. http://etext.lib.virginia.edu/etcbin/jamestown-browse?id=J1025.

Time. "Nation: The First Baker Witness." December 27, 1963. http://www.time.com/time/magazine/article/0,9171,870590,00.html#ixzz181x70IvG.

USS *Minnesota* BB-22. Rootsweb. http://freepages.military.rootsweb.ancestry.com/~cacunithistories/USS_Minnesota.html.

The Written Record of the Voyage of 1524 of Giovanni da Verrazano as recorded in a letter to Francis I, King of France, July 8th, 1524. Barnard College. http://bc.barnard.columbia.edu/~lgordis/earlyAC/documents/verrazan.htm.

ABOUT THE AUTHOR

Michael Morgan is a former Baltimore-area history teacher currently residing in Ocean City. He has been writing freelance newspaper and magazine articles on the history of the coastal region for more than three decades. His work has appeared in the *Beachcomber*, the *Maryland Times-Press* and in other newspapers in the Ocean City area. Morgan is also the author of the "Delaware Diary," which appears weekly in the *Delaware Coast Press*, and the "Sussex Journal," which is a weekly feature of the *Wave*. Morgan

Photo by Madelyn Morgan.

has also published articles in the *Baltimore Sun*, *Maryland* magazine, *Chesapeake Bay* magazine, *Civil War Times*, *World War II* magazine, *America's Civil War* and other national publications. A frequent lecturer in the coastal region, Morgan's look at history is marked by a lively storytelling style that has made his writings and lectures popular. Michael Morgan is also the author of *Pirates and Patriots: Tales of the Delaware Coast*, *Rehoboth Beach: A History of Surf and Sand* and *Bethany Beach, A Brief History*.

Visit us at
www.historypress.net